CW00660650

Annun

SALLY READ

Annunciation

~

A Call to Faith
in a Broken World

IGNATIUS PRESS   SAN FRANCISCO

Cover art:
Annunciation of Cortona
Fra Angelico (1433–1434)
Museo Diocesano, Cortona, Italy
Yorck Project, Wikimedia Commons

Cover design by Riz Boncan Marsella

© 2019 by Ignatius Press, San Francisco
All rights reserved
ISBN 978-1-62164-302-9
Library of Congress Control Number 2019931774
Printed in the United States of America ♾

To Celia Flo

In the sixth month the angel Gabriel was sent from God to a city of Galilee named Nazareth, to a virgin betrothed to a man whose name was Joseph, of the house of David; and the virgin's name was Mary. And he came to her and said, "Hail, full of grace, the Lord is with you!" But she was greatly troubled at the saying, and considered in her mind what sort of greeting this might be. And the angel said to her, "Do not be afraid, Mary, for you have found favor with God. And behold, you will conceive in your womb and bear a son, and you shall call his name Jesus.

> He will be great, and will be called the Son of the Most High;
> and the Lord God will give to him the throne of his father David,
> and he will reign over the house of Jacob for ever; and of his kingdom there will be no end."

And Mary said to the angel, "How can this be, since I have no husband?" And the angel said to her,

> "The Holy Spirit will come upon you,
> and the power of the Most High will overshadow you;
> therefore the child to be born will be called holy, the Son of God.

And behold, your kinswoman Elizabeth in her old age has also conceived a son; and this is the sixth month with her who was called barren. For with God nothing will be impossible." And Mary said, "Behold, I am the handmaid of the Lord; let it be to me according to your word." And the angel departed from her. (Luke 1:26–38)

Contents

How God comes to us; knowing Mary; the veil and the merciful gift of prayer; the Eucharist as our Annunciation: a new way of being with God; how you are longing for him and he for you; don't mistake a man for God; the importance of knowing God's eyes on you; Mary's experience, and my experience, are yours.

How anxiety shackles us; how faith keeps us whole; we are God's family—but don't be overfamiliar; the importance of intimacy and awe; how God transforms our suffering: he is the ultimate artist, and he completes everything we have the courage to begin; becoming the double-hearted Christian; how you need to give up your misery and how the Mass helps you to do it.

Who am I? Being known and being named; the mortification of the stranger; knowing that our identity is in God; knowing who Mary is helps you know who you are; how God chooses to need you—the importance of touch.

   The fiat *of motherhood and every vocation; the importance of nourishing the city of God within us; the necessity of silence; learning his word; how his language forms us; suffering with Christ; how the sacraments shape and support our lives.*

   Being (happily) wounded by God and by man; when prayers seem to go unanswered; when prayer seems impossible; choosing the path of life; another reason for the Mass —how God wants you.

Acknowledgments

Thanks are due, as always, to those who support me and advise me in my writing—particularly my husband Fabio, Tim Bete, Marie Cabaud Meaney, and Father Paul Murray. I also very much appreciate the work of all the team at Ignatius Press.

As I am poet-in-residence of the Hermitage of the Three Holy Hierarchs, my writing is always watched and prayed over by Father Gregory Hrynkiw. For that I am eternally grateful.

And thank you to Flo, for listening.

Introduction

Why?

"I don't know if I believe in God."

So said my daughter two days before her First Communion. The lacy dress was bought, the prayers learned; cousins were arriving by plane and train with envelopes of money. Her friends were lisping prayers for world peace and anticipating new iPhones, bouncy castles, and parties for a hundred.

"I want the party more than Communion. Maybe I shouldn't do it," she said.

Her first statement was literal—she *thought* she might believe in God, but how could she *know*? She felt nothing in prayer. The Mass was long and boring, and she didn't see why we had to go. I was a sad inquisitor in the lamplight by her bed—tiredly torn, like the mother of the bride when the cake has been iced and the feet have turned cold. When pressed she wouldn't say that she didn't believe in Jesus' life, death, and Resurrection; nor would she deny his divinity. I felt the surge of what the world would tell me I should say in the face of her uncertainty, and I said it:

"Don't do it. Wait a bit. Do it when you're grown up if you like."

Immediately I saw her disappointment in me. Would I let her slip away so easily? In her face I saw the panic of being let go alone, godless, in the streets outside. Simultaneously, there was a strong pain in my chest.

"The thing is, if you don't receive Communion on Sunday, Jesus will be very sad."

(As I said those words I heard, again, the voice of the world: "Manipulation! Sentiment! Blackmail!")

"He wants you, particularly *you*. He doesn't need you to know he exists in a clever way. He doesn't need you to hear his voice or see angels. What he's asking you to do is to open a door so that he can reach you better. Do you think that you could just open the door?"

It was six years since my own conversion. God came to me when my daughter was three, and almost overnight I changed the nursery narrative from "There is no God" to "He is here and I know him." I didn't make many concessions to her age when discussing these things with her: she was in her stride analyzing the nature of the Trinity (was it, she suggested, like a knife, a fork, and a spoon, each with a different function?); she welcomed a more theological take on angels and chose a Byzantine icon for her room, despite the bewildered shop assistant telling her that the cartoon cherub with blond curls was more in keeping for a little girl.

Often she would interrupt my thoughts with a question specifically relevant to what I was thinking. There is a candid photograph of the two of us arranging flower petals on the street for Corpus Christi the June before I became Catholic. We are both gazing at the petals in our hands with the same serious expression.

But the onrush of God into our lives did not shift us geographically or away from people we still held dear. Despite the fact that Flo knew the Creed in English and Italian by the age of five, I think that Catholicism will always seem fresh to her. She is what Caryll House-lander called a "rocking-horse Catholic"—a young child who converts because of a parent's conversion. Both my daughter and I are in that borderland where we can rock back and forth and easily see both worlds: new Catholic friends and old atheist ones. For all our new faith we are still close to people for whom go-ing to church is simply an odd thing to do. We know many couples who see marriage as irrelevant—apart from our gay friends, ironically. None of my daugh-ter's school friends, despite living so close to Rome, go to Mass with their families on Sundays. But she sees that I go every day. It is living in this between-space that is one of the causes of her questions.

It is also a loaded blessing having me for a mother. Little of the detail of my conversion was translated into Italian, and much was distorted on the grapevine. "Your mother saw God," a classmate told my daughter one day when she was ten. After I had explained that this was *not* the case and carefully laid out a more ac-curate version of events, she asked the inevitable ques-tion: "Why don't I feel anything during prayer?"

Like other rocking-horse Catholics, Flo is acutely aware of both the shining gift of faith and the *why* of going to Mass, the question not the answer—"Why do I *have* to go?" It may seem as though Flo became Catholic at a young age (indeed, she was baptized Catholic, to conform with societal norms, and was only four when she began going to Mass), but those earliest years of nonbelief and nonpractice are crucial to a child's development. The faith had not been transmitted to her in utero with language and love, as I have seen happen in cradle-Catholic families. She had not experienced every Sunday of her life in church from the very beginning. She knows it wasn't always like that (and besides, Dad gets to stay at home). Those four short years of not going to Mass were enough to make Sunday attendance seem an imposition, something extra we picked up along the way—unlike the brushing of teeth or bedtime reading, which at least held good through sheer, unquestioning routine.

But though my daughter's questions and sometime reluctance have been unsettling, I have come to see their genius. This borderland of doubt and dissatisfaction, need and longing is, I believe, vividly sacred ground. It is the turf of recognition and epiphany, where Nicodemus questioned Christ by night and Thomas placed his hand in his Savior's wound; where Mary Magdalene wept in almost hopelessness. It is the pinhead we can turn on, with grace. It is the edginess that cannot easily slide into indifference—indeed, it can inspire the rawest love, and its honesty and analysis are crucial to healthy faith.

What my daughter was asking for, that night before her First Communion, was a shred of proof. An angel. A reasonable proposal from God to which she could say yes. She was in that dark place where the why within us is not answered well by philosophical arguments—and certainly not by social conformity. It is the why of needing to know the essential role of God in our lives—the simple "Why bother?"; the urgency to know how he meets us in our deepest fears and desires.

Mary, the Mother of God, was always an easy entry point for us to talk about the big questions. There is a large print of Fra Angelico's *Annunciation* above the bed where she was sleeping that night, and it always fascinated her. The Annunciation holds that moment of a tipping point—the invitation and the response; the possibility of Christ in our lives or the bleakness of a world without him. Mary and Gabriel are almost like two lovers, breath held, heads bent together, as the rubrics of life are worked out and the path taken.

The Annunciation was a part of my own consciousness long before I believed in God—even then I recognized it as a pivotal encounter. I longed to find its truth and wrote numerous poems on the theme, both as the atheist that I was and more recently as a Catholic. As I was writing these pages to my daughter— her own Annunciation—I saw how those few lines of Luke contain everything of my own relationship with God, and most phases of the spiritual life: his shocking presence and invitation ("And he came to her"); the fears that he asks us to abandon ("Do not be afraid''); the realization of who we are ("Behold, I am the handmaid of the Lord'') and what our vocation might be ("Let it be to me according to your word''); and the sometime seeming absence of God ("And the angel departed from her''). Everything that Mary went through is echoed in the life of every believer—albeit distorted by our fallen nature and in lesser magnitude. Most compellingly, through Our Lady's physical reception of God, we, like her, can receive him physically in Holy Communion.

What has emerged in this book is a meditation on the universal close and remote dance with God. It is an answer to the why that we all may feel in various ways at different times and that has its genesis in the yearning that is common to mankind. Through my own experiences and those of the saints, people we know, and people I worked with long ago as a nurse,[1] I have tried to show how God moves in every moment of our lives and how without him life is so much harder.

These pages were written by a mother lovingly guiding a daughter—but they have resulted in a book that I hope will speak to anyone who has felt pain or experienced doubt, or indeed those who know well the mystery and bliss of faith. The Annunciation is an invitation to a deeper relationship with God for each and every one of us.

---

[1] Where appropriate I have changed details of stories and individuals known to me, either personally or professionally, to protect the privacy of those involved while preserving the central significance of the anecdote.

I

And he came to her (Luke 1:28)

The summer that you were six, you woke in your grandparents' house in Sardinia, whispering:

"Guess who I dreamed about!"

Your face was joyful, transformed. You bounded out of bed and downstairs. Your place was set at the head of a long table, and your grandparents sat beside you as you regaled them with the details of your vision —how the Virgin Mary had been asleep beside you in the empty bed in your room and you saw her rise, with her long brown hair loose down her back, and walk downstairs. It was a fragment—but it was vivid, and you told it with all the rapture of a seer. An aunt from next door arrived with cake and sat listening too. In the sunny, dead silence of the olive grove, beneath the stillness of the red mountains, the dream had the space to be the event that it was. Your audience lapped up every detail as though they, too, could touch something sacred. It was, perhaps, your first experience of *feeling* near to God—near to the one who is nearest.

God has many ways of coming to us. Maybe your dream was just a dream. But in your face I saw what it was that you tasted. As a young child you couldn't get enough of hearing about Mary, who came and went at Lourdes, Fatima, and Guadalupe; you couldn't get enough of hearing about angels and their visitations. You loved hearing about that afternoon meeting of the Annunciation (for I imagine it happened during the quietness of a siesta). But all those stories made you wonder, "Why does nothing happen when I pray?" and "Why does God have to be so *invisible*?"

And he came to her.

Those words are enchanting. They sound like the end of a story or the answer to a prayer. They contain the swooping relief of when God reaches out to us. There is nothing better: it is an intimation of heaven.

God does come to people, and in all kinds of ways (and the dream that lit you for so many days was, I would say, no mere accident). The Bible is full of these stories—Moses seeing the burning bush, Jacob wrestling an angel. Centuries later, Julian of Norwich was gifted with many "showings"; Saint Faustina had her visions of Christ. The list of mystical experiences is surprisingly long and inevitably varied. Of course, the "he" of the Annunciation is a messenger, the Archangel Gabriel, not God himself. But the archangels' names end with "el", which means "God", and he is etched into their nature as well[1]—so they are almost like echoes of him, one way he reaches us in extraordinary circumstances.

[1] Benedict XVI, homily, Saint Peter's Basilica, September 29, 2007.

Through history, God has sent angels (and he still does), but there was no other encounter like the Annunciation—for this particular meeting between an angel and a woman has a direct impact on your own encounter with God. It doesn't stop at the fact that Mary brought Our Lord and Savior Jesus Christ into the world. I want to show you how she solves our sometime frustration in prayer now—when we may not feel his presence, when we are stumped by the mystery, when we do not feel that he comes to us at all.

To begin with, let's think about Mary that afternoon.

When Gabriel came, she was not much older than you as I write this now. In the Fra Angelico *Annunciation* we have on the wall, she is stooped, and simple as a cutout paper doll, but the angel bows to her (she is the only nondivine person to whom an angel could bow). El Greco painted a nonchalant Mary in the face of a menacing angel with black wings. Botticelli has a fearful Mary almost pushing the angel away. There is a modern painting by the American artist John Collier where Mary is a dreamy suburban teenager wearing saddle shoes and holding a book. She could be you. But she is not Mary. Art tends not to *get* Mary. It's as if we dare not understand her too well. But if only we could try to see her as she really is, we would surely better understand how to pray.

When the angel came, it is more than probable that Mary was already praying. Long before Saint Paul's

exhortation (1 Thess 5:17), she would have been praying without ceasing. Mary is immaculate, which is another way of saying that she is exceedingly close to
God, which is another way of saying that she constantly prays. Prayer is and always was a part of her
nature, and her prayer that afternoon was the deepest
and most receptive *listening*.[2] Only she, with the Holy
Spirit, could make him flesh. It was an act of absolute, loving attention. Although Gabriel's greeting disturbed her (we will talk more about that later), there
was a kind of seamlessness with Mary's prayer and the
angel's coming. She was waiting. She was longing. She
was listening. The gravity of the angel's visit matched
the gravity of her love for God.

This kind of ceaseless prayer makes me think of
Adam and Eve before the Fall—although we can hardly
imagine how life was for our first parents. They lived
in God's gaze in a way we can't grasp. We know that
God walked in the garden (Gen 3:8) and that they
spoke with him (Gen 2:16). Digging the earth, eating
the licit fruit, talking with one another and their Creator, they lived in the warmth and the clarity of his
nearness. They were followed and they were loved—
and they knew it. There was no pain, no confusion
—they didn't have to wonder who they were, or why
they were doing what they were doing, or if it was
good enough. The lines of a blade of grass would have

[2] See Joseph Cardinal Ratzinger and Hans Urs von Balthasar,
Mary: The Church at the Source, trans. Adrian Walker (San Francisco: Ignatius Press, 2005), especially p. 72.

shivered in their minds with a profundity that we can hardly fathom.

When they were ousted from paradise, a wall went up between God and man—at least, that is how it would have felt to them: cold, concrete. Actually, people since have called it a "veil", and this is a better word —because veils can be transparent in some lights; they can move in a breeze. They don't block out communication: through them you can listen and talk. The gift of prayer is God's first work of mercy after the Fall. Millennia later, Mary, on her side, was pressed as close to the veil as she possibly could be. And in faith, she waited.

But our faith is not as perfect as hers. This veil separating you and God is still a separation. It is the cause of your sense of abandonment and your doubt (and you're far from alone in this). It was the root of your temptation to want the party (right in front of you with its visible lights and gifts) more than First Communion. It is the veil we need to try to understand.

I can imagine how empty prayer might have seemed to you as a little girl. We close our eyes, we speak some words, we get no audible answer. Perhaps we pray for something, and it doesn't seem to come to pass. You're not wrong in your sense that God is distant: we are eons away from him, across territory so dark it seems to muffle ears, eyes, and mouth. That darkness is our own consciousness of the distance we have to travel to reach him. I don't mean the physical endlessness of a long road; I mean how much we have to be purified to be with him in heaven. But through Mary, through her listening, he has given us particular ways of being close, even now.

When you were small and we went to Bungay, England, in the summer, you would hold my hand to walk the wall that borders the Saxon-towered Holy Trinity Church. We would cross the street to the grounds of Saint Mary's Church and play hide-and-seek in the ruins of the twelfth-century Benedictine priory, among the remnants of its grey stone walls and knocked-out Gothic windows. Then I would take you to wave at the gargoyles of Saint Mary's Church itself.

Saint Mary's is vast and intact. It is majestically redundant—because there are not enough Anglican believers now to keep this huge church alive as a place of worship. Like Holy Trinity and the old priory, Saint Mary's was stolen by King Henry's men during the Reformation and given to the Church of England. Henry dissolved the priory, and the fire of 1688 destroyed much of what was left of it. As we paused in the church porch, we would read the list of its prioresses dating from 1228, beginning with *Alicia*.

Inside the church, the walls are whitewashed; it is cold. Henry's men let be the devilish gargoyles outside and the griffins that stand above an emptied niche inside, but they surgically removed images of Our Lord, Our Lady, and the saints. Despite everything, the altar is mighty; above it the Ten Commandments were inscribed on the wall in the eighteenth century.

We would kneel at the long wooden altar rail close

to where nuns five hundred years before would have knelt each morning, and we would pray for them. But there is no tabernacle. I would feel as if I were praying on the tundra. There is a terrible, chilly absence, an eternal Holy Saturday. I would sit you down and explain the history of all of this to you, or try to. Then we would walk to the Catholic church next door, which was built, as soon as it was legal to do so, in the early eighteen hundreds. As we entered I would ask you to listen to the richness of the silence. We would light a candle at Mary's statue. We would genuflect before the Blessed Sacrament. Christ, in grey stone, blessed us before a crowd of angels, and we sank to our knees in his presence.

Do you feel his presence? It is a reasonable question.

One winter evening, shortly after my own First Communion, I left you at home with Dad and drove into town, alone. The black sea was visible only where it broke white, and the black sky was empty aside from a bright full moon. The town was deserted, but at the Church of San Giuseppe, Adoration was taking place. As I knelt in a pew near the front, my eyes fixed on the white Host and the words died in my head. Every prayer that I had planned vanished. I could not shift my gaze, nor could I blink. I was unable to move— that is, if I had had to move I could have done so, but it would have required an unusual effort. Yet the effort of staying absolutely still for ten minutes, twenty, was no effort at all. I had no idea of time; I seemed to be suspended.

Occasionally, I heard my own breath catch. Everything seemed to rise up in me—as though I was on the verge of laughter or shouting out for joy—but I made no sound. If it's possible, I could feel love grow as something physical within me. I felt as though I were small and had been lifted up in someone's arms: weightless.

Remember that sometimes (often) true prayer has no words; that is, always remember that words help *us*, not him. No thought, no demand, no petition is necessary. In reality, all demands and anxieties vanish in God. Time vanishes in God. There is no time in deepest prayer because we are pressed towards him, and sense, if we can be still enough, eternity. And whatever we may feel, he is lifting us and holding us still so that we can look into his eyes.

> Behold, you are beautiful, my love,
> behold, you are beautiful!
> Your eyes are doves
> behind your veil. (Song 4:1)

That winter evening in the church, before the Blessed Sacrament, God was thinning the veil. I want to say tearing away the veil, because that is how it felt. I almost cannot imagine being nearer to God in this life. The experience gave me the certainty of the completeness of heaven, its ecstasy and peace; it assured me that God will call us by our true name, and we will know perfectly that we are perfectly known, that we have always been known, always been loved, and always been seen. In Scripture it is written that angels have many eyes (Rev 4:8). The eyes of God and of his principalities are everywhere; they dwarf the cameras and screens that we focus on ourselves today in a futile attempt to feel valuable and real.

This utter motionlessness and wordlessness before the Blessed Sacrament is one kind of gift in prayer. The fact that I experienced it illustrates well that such things are unexpected (though not random) and are not necessarily given to the most holy or deserving. What these experiences do show in abundance is God's pressing back to us through the veil—or rather our *sensing him doing so*.

That night, I moved to a pew farther forward for Vespers, and I became aware of those around me: the nuns in white at the front, a young man kneeling with a rosary, an old man in a raincoat trying to stow his umbrella silently under the pew in front. No one seemed struck; no one seemed shaken.

We can never know what other people experience before the Blessed Sacrament. Some people will say they feel "nothing", and this is not wrong. In Adoration, Saint Mother Teresa of Calcutta once wrote on a piece of paper, "Father, please pray for me—where is Jesus?", and passed it to the priest at the front.[3] She,

---

[3] Paul Murray, *I Loved Jesus in the Night: Teresa of Calcutta; A Secret Revealed* (London: Darton, Longman, and Todd, 2008), p. 49.

who had had direct inspirations from God in prayer, spent decades in a dark night where she could not feel his presence. Remember: he owns the veil.

But on Holy Thursday in Santa Marinella, when the Blessed Sacrament is moved to the altar of reserve through a packed church, I often witness something else again. For that late hour, there are often very young children, dressed up in frocks or waistcoats. There are the scouts and nuns, of course, but there are also young men and women in jeans whom you may not see regularly in Sunday Mass. The church is always packed. And when the silver box containing the Blessed Sacrament is borne high by the priest, you can feel a silent urgency as people struggle to reach it—they surge, between people, around pews. There, among the white chrysanthemums and purple and yellow freesias at the side altar, people go down on their knees on the stone floor for a long time.

A teenager in a denim jacket might stand for several minutes in stricken prayer before the box. As the night goes on, a grandfather might carry in his pajamaed granddaughter and hold her on his knee before the Blessed Sacrament. It is as though we are all visiting a sickbed, a deathbed. No one seems to know how to leave. You know that these are not people who are religiously demonstrative, or demonstrative in any way, and this seems far beyond mere custom. There is heavy sobriety in the air; love and grief.

These people I see every year would probably not be described as mystics. Yet they all seem to know the reality of Jesus Christ made flesh within that box. Only four hours east of here, in Lanciano, a doubting priest experienced a Eucharistic miracle. At the words of Consecration, the bread and the wine changed into flesh and blood. These people do not seem to need the graphic nature of that miracle. They seem to understand the quiet fact of Christ's presence—at least on that particular night.

This miracle, the flesh and blood of Christ in the Eucharist, is God's way of rupturing the veil—of touching our flesh as we touch his; it is another great sign of his mercy. The week before your First Communion, I told you that receiving him would be like letting him embrace you. I can't ever ask you if you experienced any such thing. I pray you sensed something in the darkness of your body and your prayer—but *how* we perceive something doesn't change what is *there*.

When Jesus returned to Bethany after Lazarus' death, Martha rushed out into the street to beseech and reproach him, but her sister Mary stayed in the house, let down and wounded by his absence during the illness and passing of her brother. She did not understand why he had not come sooner, so she preferred to stay with her own misery in the house. Jesus called her (Jn 11:28). He called her out of her darkness, and then she went out to meet him and sank at his feet.

God does call us. He makes this gift of showing himself, of speaking, of making us understand his presence. He has done it countless times over the millennia— he did it to me. But it is an inexplicable gift. None

of us can earn it. For many, and for most of us, there
will be long periods when we do not feel his presence
and we have to content ourselves with *knowing* that he
does not leave us desolate (Jn 14:18). This is why he
left us his Body to nourish us physically (Jn 6:51–58).
This is not empty metaphor—anyone who tells you
that it is misunderstands how intimately God wants to
communicate with you. When we are sitting in a dark
room like Mary of Bethany, not comprehending the
action of God in our lives, Christ's call comes to us
through the ringing of the bell for Mass.

Think of Our Lady, that afternoon when the angel
came to her. It is because of that girl's steady faith and
listening at the other side of the veil that you, too, can
bring him physically into yourself. Every Communion
is its own Annunciation: the angels are present; you
give your attention and trust and consent to do his
will; his physical presence comes to abide in you.

The world didn't break open when Mary said yes
—but that doesn't mean she didn't conceive the Son
of God. I doubt that the birds left their places on the
trees. If someone spoke to her, I doubt in that moment
that she would have heard him.

Give God a piece of that stillness. Give him your listening. And *know* what is happening even if you don't
feel it, even if the world isn't set on fire. Mary is handing him to you. She, through God, has broken the
veil in a new way, one that doesn't require any kind of
clever prayer or florid mysticism. She has given you

his simple presence. It is in the quiet form of a circle of bread.

~

My love, you are not the only one who suffers when you feel distant from God—he suffers too. He wants you with him. This is not a long-distance relationship gone tepid. This is two people constantly searching for each other and longing for union. And just as I have talked of God's action and the ways he comes to us, you, too, are searching. And the more you search, the closer to him you will ultimately be.

Yes, Mary is immaculate, but with her you share something vital that all the saints possess: an enormous and intensely desiring heart. I first realized this through looking back to your early Christmases, and mine.

Your English grandparents were not religious at all, but your grandmother loved Christmastime, and not a single room in our cottage went undecorated. She would make yards of paper chains, licking and sticking, and pin them to our old wooden beams. The tree was always so tall that it bent where it touched the ceiling, and the coming of Santa Claus was so real to me that I vomited in excitement one Christmas morning. But nothing dwarfed the pile of presents that filled the pillowcases we left by the fireplace. It was the sheer copiousness of packages that thrilled me. My third Christmas I carried all my new toys to a corner of the playroom and sat guarding them with your uncle's toy gun.

It wasn't the contents that interested me; it was the incredible fact of their existence.

So when you came along, I made your Christmases as near to my own as I possibly could: twinkling lights, miraculous icing-sugar footprints across the floor on Christmas morning, and a mountain of presents that caused you, as a two-year-old, to fall to your chubby knees in awe.

Then, at five or six, you began to speak of a sadness on Christmas night—it was all over for another year, and you were extremely tired after all the excitement. But it became evident, too, that the longing you felt wasn't for toys; that your list to Santa (which came to include "a four-poster bed" and "a cloud") was about the furthest reaches of your heart, and presents simply failed to fill it.

You see, your heart is a vast and quite frightening thing. It was designed for God, and so, like a vertiginous and beautifully carved stone cathedral, it cries out to be filled with a voice, with love; it aches to be animated by a Spirit large enough. When you were a baby, my presence often contented you wholly (though, even then, there were nights of unexplained grief when I could not console you). But as you grew, the cathedral of your heart needed more. At first the desire was for toys, acres of bright plastic; but you soon realized that they sat in a heap in a corner of this structure and made no impact at all.

Remember the woman who met Jesus at the well, the one who had had five husbands? She was thirsty

—not just for water but for peace and love, for something that would not make her say when she sank into a chair at the end of the long day, "Is there nothing else?"

> Whoever drinks of the water that I shall give him will never thirst. (Jn 4:14)

God quenches our thirst. God fills the cathedral of our hearts. We no longer need company for the sake of company; we don't need an endless supply of toys, bags, shoes, or alcohol.

That insatiability that you felt as a child on Christmas Day is evidence of a heart made for God. It is that insatiability that can, if misdirected, lead to alcoholism or obsessive love in any of us. When you were little and became overtired and discontent you would say, "I want to go home."

"We *are* home!" we would all cry. But I knew the yearning behind the words—you were longing for the happiness only God can give, of completion and peace.

It's not just you and the woman at the well who are longing. Mary at the Annunciation was longing too. We're used to seeing images of Mary as replete, even vapid. I dispute them. I say she was on fire with longing. Some of the earliest accounts of the Annunciation say that Mary went out with a jug to fetch water[4]— just like the Samaritan woman. And Mary, too, was longing for her God, because the physical Christ had

---

[4] Protoevangelium of James, quoted in Ratzinger and von Balthasar, *Mary*, p. 94.

not yet entered her life. God could embed himself in Mary precisely because she was yearning so intensely for him. Her genius of sanctity was in knowing the vastness of her own heart and knowing that only God could fill it.

This knowledge is the goal of every alcoholic in Alcoholics Anonymous; it should be the objective of every person who thinks a relationship will fulfill him entirely; it is the antidote to believing that money or power will complete us. If the world had this knowledge, it would mean the cessation of violence and war.

Like the Samaritan woman, you will very likely fall in love (my heart quakes at the thought). You will sleep, but your heart will be awake (Song 5:2). You will rise from your bed and seek him. You will think of him day and night. He will be the first thought of the morning, and the last thought before you sleep; you will dream of him all night. Some of us fall far, long before we meet the person we are supposed to spend the rest of our life with, and any kind of love— like money or alcohol—can try to lay claim, falsely, to the vast expanse of our hearts.

I first fell in love when I was fifteen—or thought I did. He was nineteen. He introduced me to Stanislavsky and J. D. Salinger and gave me another life separate from my schoolgirl existence. When, after three months, he ended the relationship, I was broken. Even then I knew what my devastation consisted of: when he disappeared he took his idealized perception of me with him. More than that, he trashed it. He had been mistaken. Even then, at fifteen, I recognized it was not *him* I missed—his big brown eyes and endless jokes. I felt as though he had destroyed my *self*. He had held up a mirror and created an image of me that I believed in. It was the first time I had consciously seen myself reflected in someone else's eyes. He had thought me beautiful—no more. He had thought me fascinating —no more. "The mirror crack'd from side to side." Like the Lady of Shalott imprisoned in her tower,[5] I was forced to look at reality, which for me meant a world without my lover's capricious gaze, and also without God. I thought it would destroy me.

This is why it is important to remember: any earthly love is only ever the barest intimation of your love for God and his for you. Remember that no man will know you as God does—and therefore no man will define you, save you, or break you. When you feel the intense pain of something or someone on this earth enslaving you, remember, *that* is your searching for God. *That* is your immense heart looking to be filled. But the immensity of your heart is made for and can be filled entirely only by the breadth and length and height and depth of God (Eph 3:18). Once you

[5] The poem "The Lady of Shalott" by Alfred Lord Tennyson tells the tale of a woman imprisoned in a tower in Arthurian England, condemned to look at the outside world only through a mirror. When she sees the beauty of Lancelot, she turns to look at him directly, and the mirror cracks. She sails alone down the river to her doom. Ironically, it is Lancelot who, on seeing her corpse, implores God to give her grace—something she clearly missed in life.

recognize this, you will feel him come to you: it is the sudden knowledge of knowing someone you cannot see is there in the darkness.

When it seems that God is distant, it is vital to remember his gaze. When Mary of Bethany hid in the darkness of her house, she knew that Christ was outside. She may have doubted in those moments, she may not have understood what he was doing, but she knew that his gaze was on her—*and he came to her.* He knew her longing and her distress. Ultimately, he did not disappoint her.

Prayer is practicing the knowledge of God's eyes upon you. He is the only one who should act as your mirror. Prayer should be God's gaze drenching you, as the rain drenches the grasses in the garden, vivifying their greens and making them stand taller. God's gaze awakens you to everything you were created to be. It enables you to leave the darkness and to walk to him.

It seems to me that as people pray less, the need to be gazed at becomes more. People photograph every frame of their life: the fact of it happening and resounding in their own heart is not enough. As soon as something happens—an engagement, a holiday—we tell it to the audience of social media. We package it. It is like being given a flower and pressing it instantly into immortality so the juice and scent are gone. Perhaps people don't know that this is also about searching for God, about being *seen* in a world that denies his eyes. The messages we post are often blanket, indiscriminate. Social media has removed the niceties of how we frame a message for different people: if we're announcing a pregnancy it should be done gently to the woman who wants children but has none, more enthusiastically to grandparents.

But how would it feel to have an experience and not to post it, not to share it? How would it feel to fall in love, accept a proposal of marriage, and not tell anyone—at least at first? I think people are afraid. They think that experiences are not real unless they have an audience. They are scared of the overwhelming silence in the cathedral of their hearts.

> But Mary kept all these things, pondering them in her heart. (Lk 2:19)

What happens to us needs to mature in silence. It needs to take root in us and therefore become unshakable. It needs to find its place in the Reality of God. Because only then, in the illuminating context of the Creator's gaze, can we understand what something *is* and how it relates to everything else. We need to understand that we have worth without an audience; that we should not measure ourselves by the world's criteria: money, numbers, and what plays well to the crowd.

When you are waiting for God to come to you (life is waiting for God, though more accurately he is waiting for you), always know that his gaze is your spiritual oxygen, your context, and truth.

> O LORD, you have searched me and known me!
> You know when I sit down and when I rise up;
> you discern my thoughts from afar.

You search out my path and my lying down,
and are acquainted with all my ways.
Even before a word is on my tongue,
behold, O LORD, you know it altogether.
You beset me behind and before,
and lay your hand upon me. (Ps 139:1–5)

~

The evening before your First Communion when you wondered why and felt God's distance so acutely, my answers may have made little impression on you. But you did go forward and open the door to Christ, and I will never forget the expression on your face as you walked back across the lawn after receiving him, to take your seat. The May day was sunny, the same date as the First Communion of Saint Thérèse of Lisieux, and the priest read aloud from Thérèse's own recollections.

I remember hearing her certainty and, with a smile, comparing it with your hesitation. But while you may have wobbled the night before your big day, it seems to me that this was mainly because you understood the gravity of what would take place.

Notwithstanding the commonality of religious experience, we all sense God in different ways, at different points in our lives. He speaks to us all in particular ways, like a father with many children, all of whom need a slightly different style of parenting. He is the opposite of social media, with its sledgehammer proclamations. He will come to you when and in the way that is best for you. He will give you knowledge of him to the extent that you are capable of bearing it. (Who among us, now, could stand before the perfect face of God? We would burn up in his beauty. The faults in us would blacken and burn like tissue paper against a flame.) He even withholds his consolations for certain people in ways that bring out their most heroic best (think of the extraordinary mission of Saint Mother Teresa of Calcutta through her dark night; think of her now, so close to God). And remember, too, that credible private revelation (or "mystical experience") is never just for the person who receives it. Julian of Norwich stressed this,[6] and we take comfort from her visions and feel closer to God because of them. He chose to speak through *her* to reach *us*.

I think one of our greatest errors is in thinking that we are quite alone in our relationship with God. Of course, in one sense, we are just that: intensely alone with our Creator. But in another sense, we are more connected to each other—to family, to friends, to previous generations and generations to come, to the whole of humanity—than we can ever realize here on this earth. Mary's experiences are also yours, and she prays for you. My conversion belongs to you too. Every valid experience in prayer, every message received is meant for every Christian. Your grandfather's God-

[6] See chap. 8 in *Revelations of Divine Love Recorded by Julian, Anchoress at Norwich*, trans. Grace Warrack, Project Gutenberg EBook, September 2, 2016.

less life is yours, and so is his skepticism and his cyni-
cism. He never knew you. But your prayers in a house
that he never imagined can touch the days of his life
twenty-five, forty, sixty years ago, as an opening of
grace that we cannot quantify or understand. Mary's
prayers that quiet afternoon reach like a river to millennia ahead: they bring you to her Son.

In the meantime, when you feel spiritually cold, wait
like Mary of Bethany for his call. Know that you exist
in his gaze. He will come to you, because you were
made for that. It's true that he is very far away. But the
beauty is this: Christ is with us on our journey. He
came to us to lead us back to the Father. He is walking with you in your blindness and your feeling of not
being heard. Like Mary our Mother, accept him physically into the depths of yourself in Communion—for
this is no metaphor. A priest once told me that every
Communion is a mystical experience. It is true: our
Mother said yes to her own extraordinary encounter
so that you can encounter him too.

2

Do not be afraid (Luke 1:30)

When you are grown up and reading this, will you remember how many times I told you as a child, "Do not
be afraid"? That, and "Don't worry" and "I love you."
Sometimes they are interchangeable. "I love you," I
will say before the math test, meaning "Do not be
afraid."

"What if I fail?" you say.

And I answer, "Don't worry."

God tells us not to be afraid repeatedly through
Scripture (Dan 10:12; Is 41:10; 1 Jn 4:18) and continues to tell us so through private revelation (Julian
of Norwich, Saint Faustina). If, for mothers, "Do not
be afraid" is another way of saying "I love you", it has
to be much the same way with God. It cannot mean
"Bad things won't happen one hundred percent." It
means "My love is part of you, it will sustain you, and
my infinitely consoling arms are there for you at the
end of the day."

It doesn't stop life from being scary. Any given day
(especially a day with an angelic appearance and a seemingly impossible commission from God) can seem a
series of insurmountable obstacles. "Just get past the

math test and you're on the home stretch," I say to you. But every moment of every day, however uneventful, is a gentle query that awaits your answer.

Long before you were born, I trained to be a psychiatric nurse, and I worked for a few weeks at an old asylum in London. The memory is as dingy and indistinct as the place itself, and I remember none of the patients I nursed there. But what I have always remembered is a patient I didn't nurse. He was a young man who had the name of a bird—or perhaps it was a foreign name that sounded like a bird. Anyway, I will call him "Crow".

Crow was kept at the top of the building in a contained suite, with its own living room, bedroom, and bathroom. Two nurses were with Crow twenty-four hours a day. They were not simply present with Crow: they each physically had Crow by an arm. As he raised his fork from his plate to his mouth, a nurse's arm would raise too. As he scratched his nose, the nurse's hand was there too. Crow was not alone even in the bath or when asleep at night. Most of the time, the two very bored nurses and Crow sat in a sad line, arms linked, watching daytime television. You see, Crow was suicidal—but it wasn't the usual kind of danger-to-self that we were used to, the kind that warranted checks every half hour, ten minutes, or five minutes; the kind that meant hiding sharp objects and keeping windows locked. Crow compulsively sought an exit. Left alone to clean his teeth, he would ram the toothbrush down his throat. Left alone in the bath, he would try to swallow the plug. Left alone to eat, he would jam the fork into the electric socket or try to poke out an eye.

As student nurses we were bewildered. To begin with, anyone serious about killing himself did not behave like this. And, as any lover of sentimental songs knows, loving means letting go. The constant hand-holding had become a behavioral pattern that seemed impossible to break.

I don't know how long that situation lasted, whether it was fixed with behavioral therapy or drugs. I only heard the grim details of the story from a succession of student friends who were sent to work up there, to bring Crow his food, or to make coffee for the nurses holding onto his hands like two noonday shadows.

What I was left with was an image of a bird-boy who would fly from the window of life given a sliver of a chance.

Crow was frightened. Every moment that God presented to him was rejected. How light his arms would have felt if the nurses had let him go. How dizzying his freedom if he had walked down the corridor and out into the street.

"Do not be afraid", someone might say to him. And, like you, he might say:

"What if I fail?"

Perhaps now I see Crow as a child who resists dropping his mother's hand and doesn't want to sleep by himself.

I am like a lonely bird on the housetop. (Ps 102:7)

Mary's steady aloneness at the scene of the Annunciation is so very different from Crow's enforced companionship. It is fear that makes us birdlike and skittish. Our hearts hammer, our thoughts will not settle, we fly from one project to another, unable to go deeper, unable to be still. Fear can make us reject the moment. It can make us fly from the exam, the competition; in the most pathological cases, like Crow's, from life itself. Given a life-changing proposal, confusing news, upset, what do we do? Like Jonah when God told him to go to Nineveh, we may run in the opposite direction. Or we may freeze.

Mary did not run, nor did she vacillate. Her openness to the present moment placed Christ in all his glory within her. The Hebrew word for "glory" means "weight", and I see the unborn Christ growing within his mother as a weight that, with every shred of her consent, pinned Mary to this world and the work that God gave her. As ballast balances a ship, Christ within us gives us the steadiness that makes us know who we are and how to accept the present moment as divine will.[1] Unlike Crow, who was fixed here by human hands, Mary was held to the moment through the love of God.

---

[1] Read *Abandonment to Divine Providence* by Jean-Pierre de Caussade. It will teach you that embracing each moment is the best way to cling to Christ.

Without the weight of God binding us to this world, we risk flying into pieces.

Just after your great-grandparents and your grandfather had died within a few months of each other, I was living alone in an attic in London. One night, I woke to pitch-blackness and quite literally did not know *who* I was. Of course, we all wake sometimes not knowing *where* we are, especially if we are travelling. But I did not know if I was a woman or a man, young or old, whether I had children, what my life was at all. I saw myself as bald and faceless, and I seemed to thrash about in the darkness for something to grasp. Finally a thought came to me—my studies. From there, hand over hand, I pieced together my work as a nurse, the fact I had no children, my age. And my *self* fell back into my consciousness. But I was sweating with fear.

This too is anxiety of the most existential kind, and it can happen at the points in life when we face the big dislocations, the points at which, to those who have faith, the veil between us and God is thinnest. I mean death, birth, growing up, heartbreak, or any kind of violent change. At these junctures, we are at most risk of fragmenting or running away from the present moment that God wills for us. Sometimes through these periods, the way that we see the world can warp —because in our panic *we are trying to write the moment ourselves*; we are trying to circumvent pain. People who are slender can truly believe they are fat, and all of their psychic energies go on that phantom. People become addicted to drink or drugs. People can become convinced that they are the opposite sex. Or that they have a disease. We often create a fictitious world to inhabit. The fiction is sometimes more painful than the reality.

Faith keeps us whole and in touch with what is real. We know that we are part of a much larger story that begins from before our birth (Jer 1:5) and extends to long after our death. No matter how alone you may feel, you are held by God and are known more thoroughly than you know yourself. When you see the world as a child of God, you will find that this vision binds you to the world, where he has placed you, in the person he created—*yourself*.

Sanctity does not necessarily give immunity to mental illness. Mental suffering, like physical suffering, is a part of the human condition and can be a part of our redemption. But faith can and does reduce anxiety— I cite my own experience. It made me realize *who I am* (we'll come to that) and the context in which I exist (as we said, God's gaze). It helped me to accept that I cannot control all the events of life, no matter how many lists I make, or how many nights I stay awake rehearsing an infinite number of scenarios in my head. Keep in mind: the frightening moment that you fear will completely overwhelm you is not yours to fall apart over. It belongs to God, and so do you (Ps 100:3). Let him lead you through it.

～

Mary stayed steady. Just think: Gabriel's news would have unhinged most of us. But Mary held together. There is another reason for this, quite apart from (though connected to) the glory of God within her and her total acceptance of the present moment. It is about the way that God spoke to her on that day. And this affects the way that you speak to him now.

Imagine the fear that anyone would feel at the sight of the muscular, colorful Gabriel of Renaissance art swaggering into the yard. It's easy to assume that his very appearance made Mary jump out of her skin. But in fact, we don't know in what form he appeared to her. It probably was not as the angel appeared to Daniel in the Old Testament, with a face like lightning and eyes of flaming torches (Dan 10:6). Daniel, understandably, fell to the ground. As did Joshua (Josh 5:14). Zechariah was "troubled . . . and fear fell upon him" (Lk 1:12) at the sight of Gabriel hovering smokily beside the altar. Lot (Gen 19:1) bowed deeply before the presence of angels, whose appearance was perhaps more like that of ordinary men. Hagar, another woman, met her angel going out to the well (again) and seems to have been poised at the encounter; yet even she wonders how she has seen him and remained alive (Gen 16:13).

We don't know how Gabriel looked to Mary, but we know she reacted differently from those who collapsed or shook. When she first became aware of him, she may have experienced that jolt of the partial rupturing of the veil between God and mankind. But at no point does she bow down, let alone fall down. Nevertheless, Gabriel notices that she is greatly "troubled" (or "perplexed" in some translations) by his greeting—by his *greeting*, notice, not his appearance; God wanted *all* of Mary's attention on his plan, and he does not floor the girl with a visual display—and he reassures her, "Do not be afraid." Again and again through Scripture, God says those words to us.

I want you to think about Mary's relative calm and how she gathered herself to interrogate the angel and consent to the words that came after. Among all the people in Scripture who had meetings with angels, Mary stands out as being one of the most composed, especially when we consider that *she* is the one from whom most is asked. Consider her quick thinking— her question "How can this be" (Lk 1:34; meaning, "How shall this be?") coupled with her forthright consent. This is a clear-eyed encounter.

Mary's sanctity, her trust, and her childlike nature allow her (after her initial disturbance) a curious ease with which to be so intimate with God that afternoon. Think again about those words: "How can this be, since I have no husband?", and remember Zechariah's words (just a little earlier in Luke) when the angel (the same angel) tells him that Elizabeth will conceive: "How shall I know this? For I am an old man, and my wife is advanced in years" (Lk 1:18). They're similar thoughts. One might say they are both reasonable queries. But Gabriel strikes terrified Zechariah dumb for his lack of trust, while he explains with perfect patience to young Mary the workings of what will happen. The juxtaposition of these two angelic conversations is no coincidence. God is showing us a beautiful new collaboration with humanity. He is gentle with Mary; she is calmly bold with God.

One day, you will go alone to the National Gallery in London. Find the Sainsbury Wing, and among the lofty wood-shined rooms of medieval and Renaissance Madonnas, you will see Fra Lippi's *Annunciation*. It will be at your height, and you will see the frame arching over Mary and Gabriel, both bowing their heads in mutual respect. They are two people intent on something; they are frozen at that moment of his proposal. Look to the ground underneath them: every daylily is exquisite: ivory and veined with grey. They look as I imagine the flowers must have looked to Eve in Eden, each petal crying out the beauty of its form. Everything hangs in the balance in this painting. To me, it is the most perfect Annunciation because it, more than all the others, illustrates the nexus of this new relationship between God and man: collaboration; the possibility of balance between the human and the divine.

Through her conception and pregnancy, Mary is physically touched by God—and remains standing! She becomes his Mother, and through this we became his adoptive children. We are family: her ease, her familiarity with God are passed to us. As in any family, the love should be unconditional. As in any family, there is a risk of taking people for granted.

It makes me think of how, during Mass, you used to slouch and yawn during the Eucharistic Prayer. "*Why* do we have to go to Mass?" you would ask me on a Sunday morning; "I don't get it." And that casual neglect didn't make you unique: other people slouch, some don't kneel; let's face it, a lot of people aren't even there. Which makes me think again of Jonah and *his* reaction to the pressing presence and demands of God: he ran away. Running from God doesn't necessarily mean bolting to Tarshish. It can mean not looking at what's happening on the altar, not praying, staying home to be on social media. Why should we show up?

If only we truly understood that Christ is present on the altar, we would throw ourselves to the ground as Daniel did at the sight of the angel. We might cover our faces as Moses did before the burning bush.

Or would we?

Through our new covenant with God, through Jesus Christ, it has all become so easy. We show up; he's there. We can take him in our hand like a cookie. God on a plate for us. Isn't this the modern way? God is our chum. He wouldn't ever demand something old-fashioned or difficult, like respect or self-control.

If that is your thinking, you have trashed the greatest inheritance you will ever receive. This, really, is the downfall of the modern world—to be so familiar with God that we forget to love him, to honor him, to worship him.

Even to believe in him. (Because who could truly believe in any God that doesn't command respect?) He comes to us as one of us, with one of us as his Mother. But we should never forget what the Incarnation signifies: the sublime ineffability, the omnipotence, the wonder and glory of the triune God. Don't let modernity fool you; spend some time with Moses and Daniel to understand the awe that we should feel. God took a great risk in sending himself as man; one might almost say he trusted us. He trusted dear Mary, the level-headed girl who listened that afternoon. Repay his trust by loving him so hard that you could swoon.

For knowing how to behave before God, Mary, as usual, is your best model. She was recollected that day, not casual; she was troubled, but she didn't run. Perhaps, for all of us, every Communion contains Mary's initial wariness: How can this be? Is God himself contained in this wafer, in this wine? We should be steady, like Mary, look him in the eye and receive with great attention and reverence. But when we return to our place to pray, we might ask ourselves, like Hagar, "How can it be that I have touched God and lived?" (cf. Gen 16:13).

He slips into us with the ease with which he slipped into Mary (we owe this to her courageous consent), but our own response, our own recollection, is crucial. Be quiet in the darkness of your body with him.

If he chooses to speak, now is the easiest time for you
to hear. That doesn't mean words (though some have
heard them); it means the branding of a message on
your heart; its sense might be wordless, but it is inescapable.

Your mind might attach words to that message quickly,
so you will remember it. That is all right. Sometimes your mind provides words too quickly, and you'll
know deep down that they are not from God. Knowing the difference—what comes from God and what
from you—is not too hard; it is the difference between
your mind preparing a phrase to speak and your ears
receiving a sound with no warning.[2] In those moments
after Communion, you will find that thoughts that go
against his will do not come or do not come easily.
Shut out the whispers of your friends on either side
of you. Shut out your boredom and frustration. Know
intimacy; know awe. He should find a hollowness in
you that only he can fill.

~

"I don't want to be a Christian," you told me when
you were six and disconcerted by the riveting stories
that I was reading you in the evenings, of saints being
beheaded or eaten by lions.

Terrible things happened to Mary too. Those words,
"Do not be afraid", reverberated not only through the

[2] Saint Teresa of Avila uses this method of distinction when
writing about interior locutions in chapter 25 of her autobiography.

Annunciation but through all the rest of Mary's life —through her disruptive pregnancy and exile, as the mother of an unusual child, as mother to an even more unusual adult, as witness to his hounding, scourging, and torture, and being nailed to a cross; and into her eternal existence in heaven, where she labors for the conversion of everyone.

Why *not* be afraid? one might ask.

For a time you truly thought that being a Christian meant suffering more than most. As a child you quickly saw that being a believer doesn't necessarily mean a jolly, comfy existence.

So what can the words "Do not be afraid" really mean? And if God wills every moment, does he will the terrible things too?

Long ago in a poor, small town on a Sardinian hillside, a young priest was asked to take over the parish. The decrepit church was halfway up a steep hill and hemmed in by mountains. The townspeople were wanting, wayward, and given to solving their differences with violence. There was (some say there still is) a belief in the darkly pagan, in curses and such, that ran alongside a lively faith. The young priest happened to be an artist, and he set to designing a large and impressive Romanesque church to replace the existing one. The plans were outsize for that kind of a town. Those that knew of his intentions said, frankly, that it could not be done. But the priest sold everything that he and his family possessed and begged alms until he could, unbelievably, build it. It took years. Everything about the church was designed by him, even down to the candleholders. He sculpted a beautiful Madonna and the Stations of the Cross in stone, and he painted a fresco of Mary being assumed into heaven, high above the altar.

The priest was a holy man, and his piety and dedication drew in the townspeople. Faith seemed to reign in the company of this unlikely beauty and its small maker. The town still talks of him, his example and kindness; how he created with the patient tenderness and dedication of a gardener.

He began drawing frescoes of saints in the tall side altars, along with the Immaculate Conception and the Pietà. Apparently, he wasn't content with his interpretation of the Assumption above the altar and wanted to change it, but first he worked long hours up a ladder, sketching his frescoes in charcoal. By the end of summer, he had completed and painted Saint Sebastian, but the other images were only drafted in black, faceless or with sketchy features, still not quite ready for painting.

It was a September day. Some say the young priest was taken out for lunch by parishioners at the end of the morning. I imagine him coming down from his ladder, tired and in need of food. Later, when he returned to the church, he felt ill. A doctor was called, but the priest said he had no need of a physician: he needed the doctor of his soul. A neighboring father arrived; the young priest made his confession and died straight afterwards.

The frescoes were never finished.

You know that church and how its Romanesque arches provide the perfect acoustics for pipes and song. The nave is dominated by the enormous incomplete drawings on the walls, which are as they were on the day that the young priest died. (Those people will never touch the projects of the dead.) They are simple, ghostly shapes of images we know well: the dead Christ on his Mother's lap; Mary with her hands outstretched. In front of them the parish has placed smaller, finished artworks on the same themes, to help people recognize what the sketches were going to be.

But in their very incompleteness the sketches seem to speak far louder of their artist than they would have if they had been finished. The walls of the church are spectral, but the lines of the sketches crackle with life. We seem to see the priest's hands at work in them. We feel his desire to see the church painted with devotional scenes in the very fact that this did not happen in the way that he intended. We can almost hear his sigh.

To many the story is simply tragic, even pathetic—a confirmation of life's futility. Why would God not allow the completion of this man's simple plans? Did God will him to die so prematurely—a much-loved parish priest who united and inspired the town?

Illness, obstacles, and death were ushered into the world by Adam and Eve when they grasped at power and knowledge beyond them. Suffering and death sometimes seem to swarm around the world like serpents, indiscriminate in when or whom they bite. God can intervene. Sometimes God does intervene. One thing we can be sure of: not one thing happens that is not sanctioned by him (even if it pains us; even if it pains *him*; even if its motive is infinitely mysterious to us). He *is* in everything.

> We know that in everything God works for good with those who love him, who are called according to his purpose. (Rom 8:28)

Stepping into the silent church and seeing the thoughts and plans of this man on the walls—the shape of Mary without a face—is to witness how God completes our incompletion. We think we can finish a story, but we are only players in a far-larger work. We never actually finish anything. The unfinished drawings of our lives reach up to the greater Creator. Think back to Crow. His fear was also the fear of simply beginning. We share this fear, you and I. It's a kind of perfectionism: what if what I create isn't brilliant, what if no one likes it, what if I'm ranked sixth or seventh instead of first? Read Jesus' parable of the talents (Mt 25:14–30). Burying what you have been given in the dirt is not an option. Fear is a kind of sin because it shows we are not trusting God. Be sure that he will use whatever you do even if, in the world's eyes, it doesn't seem successful. You can never dream how God will use anything that you may have the courage to begin.

The priest-artist's is a sad story, but gentle, isn't it? I know, at six, that you were more worried about being chased up trees by cannibals. And, like everyone else, as you grow, you worry about disease, disaster, war, the inescapable brutality of existence. Pain something like Christ's pain; pain like Mary's pain under the cross.

We live in an age marked by the overwhelming aim of avoiding pain. Painkillers are often taken at the barest onset of a headache. Women (understandably) ask for epidurals to deaden labor. We even kill the child within us if we feel he will bring on more suffering than we think we could ever manage. We even kill ourselves, or our loved ones, if we feel that our or their suffering is too great. Suffering is indeed a terrible thing—and avoiding it can obviously be humane and justifiable. But it can also be in the very avoidance of pain that we unleash yet more of it.

As a nurse I met a lot of people who were busy avoiding suffering. There was the woman whose husband had left her and whose daughter had moved thousands of miles away, who rarely left the house. She wouldn't risk new friendships, new loves, and grief. She sat, white-knuckled in the chair all day, holding on to what remained. The weight piled on, her skin became mottled, her breathing labored. Soon, even walking down the garden path scared her too much.

I think of another woman I knew whose life looked disappointing. She hadn't managed to go to college or get a good job. She was stuck in the small town of her childhood, and she knew the heavy pain of boredom. She soon turned to cannabis to paint the days more interesting colors—and it worked for a while. Then, one day, she was offered something stronger to embellish life. She took it and quickly became addicted. The pain piled on. I think of the plight of her firstborn, addicted to heroin and going through withdrawal in an incubator, wearing his tiny knitted cap.

I think of a friend who, at forty-seven, is very alone. She has had a lifetime of lovers and more than one pregnancy. But she aborted those children, as she could not see how she would cope with them as a single mother. It is a terrible thing to see the face of a woman who has had no children and now desperately wants them, considering, for a fleeting moment over coffee, the fact that she has ended the life of more than one child in her womb.

You see, if we run from suffering (and especially if we sin as we run), our troubles can become darker, deeper, and more tangled. Heaven knows that I, too, have the tendency to run from legitimate pain. But we must try to remember: suffering itself is unavoidable.

Do Gabriel's words mean that Mary did not suffer? No.

Tradition says that Mary did not feel pain while giving birth to Jesus. As a woman free from sin, she did not feel the pains brought on by the Fall. That same tradition might make some think that she did not feel fear or grief under the cross.

But she most certainly did feel fear and grief—after all, she was immaculate, not lobotomized. As a fully human person she experienced the full gamut of human emotion, without sin. We know she suffered worry as any mother would, when young Jesus was missing for three days (Lk 2:48). We can conclude that she felt pain under the cross. Sanctity, sadly, does not immunize anyone from pain.

You grew up familiar with an extraordinary face: a beautiful young woman with a luminous smile and an eye patch covering one eye. You saw her on my phone and on the cover of books. She lived quite near us, though we didn't know her, and she died when you were six. She will almost certainly be canonized by the Church.

Chiara Corbella's life was full of terribly bad luck, one could say. She fell pregnant shortly after getting married, but an early scan showed that the baby girl had anencephaly. Chiara and her husband, Enrico, knew from the beginning that they would not abort the child as they were advised to do but instead would "accompany" her as far as they could. Maria was born naturally and lived for forty minutes, during which time she was baptized. Despite losing her so quickly, both parents said that they felt blessed in the incredible gift of being with her through her earthly life. The shortness of the minutes following the birth did not diminish that gift.

Chiara quickly became pregnant again. Initial scans showed that this baby, a boy, did not have the same condition as his sister. But later tests revealed that he had a vanishingly rare syndrome that rendered him, too, "incompatible with life". Once again, Chiara carried him until he was born naturally. Like his sister, he was baptized immediately and died less than an hour later.

Chiara then became pregnant a third time. This time the baby in utero was shown to be absolutely healthy. But during the pregnancy Chiara developed an ulcer on her tongue that would not go away. It turned out to be cancer. She had a choice: begin treatment and lose the baby, or wait and risk the treatment being too late. She chose to save her baby's life and began treatment after his birth. She died when he was a year old.

Chiara Corbella was filmed after the death of her first child, giving testimony at a pro-life conference.[3] She speaks about having the scan of Maria and receiving the news that the baby would not survive. That day Chiara was alone; her husband could not be with her. She says that she wondered why—why would God ask her to receive this news by herself, meaning that she would have the added pain of telling Enrico? Then she reflected that Mary was alone at the Annunciation. The news, the moment, was all hers, at least for a time.

What strikes me most watching the film of Chiara is the range and play of emotion on her face. There is nothing unstable about her—yet she cries freely; she smiles, luminously, too. She speaks of the exquisite joy of holding Maria after she was born. There is pain; there is also genuine happiness. How can this possi-

[3] "Nel mondo ma non del mondo—Scienza e vita (1)—Chiara Corbella Petrillo'', YouTube, uploaded October 8, 2012, https://www.youtube.com/watch?v=ZX-gFbtC2dU.

bly be? We're told that even after the deaths of both her first two babies, and contemplating her own, she —though frightened and sad—was still radiant with some kind of joy.

Back in 1974, Pope Paul VI talked about Christians having a double heart—one natural, one supernatural.[4] What afflicts us here, in this life, doesn't have to cancel out the bliss that is unleashed within us knowing that God is with us and loves us and that life extends beyond the here and now. Chiara was a little like the Sardinian priest at the top of his ladder, trying to finish the work that he rightly believed that God gave to him. Chiara was at the top of a similar ladder, handing her babies, and then herself, over to God. She wasn't in control of her life. She could not look after her first two babies for long, and ultimately she couldn't look after her one surviving child. But God completes her work, as he completes the priest's.

"How can I pray when there is so much suffering in the world?" you once protested when you were little. The reason for Chiara's supernatural heart—her joy in the midst of suffering—was that her face was pressed tight against the veil in prayer. The fact that Chiara recognized that the length of her children's brief lives did not detract in any way from the unforgettable grace that they were, shows us that she was able to see, in the most partial way, with the eyes of God. "Whatever

[4] Paul VI, General Audience (June 26, 1974).

you do will have sense only if you see it in terms of eternal life,'' she wrote in a letter to her third child,[5] whom she would leave behind when she died.

This deep and lived understanding of eternity shows that she was blessed with a profound knowledge of God; and this knowledge was born of the deepest, most authentic love. Truly loving God means becoming more like him (Rom 13:14). This, then, can allow us some gift of divine intuition. She was given a spirit of wisdom and revelation (Eph 1:17–18) through love. Chiara demonstrates why, in the face of all suffering, we have no valid alternative to prayer.

Of all the pictures we have seen of Mary there is barely one that looks like I imagine her to be. The Botticellis are beautiful, but a little precious. Some of the Leonardos look downright unhealthy. I don't even know, really, what I expect to see in a portrait of Our Lady: Courage? Youth? Wisdom? Suffering? Serenity? But in that short piece of film, in the play of emotion on Chiara's young face, I see something of what I might expect Mary to look like.

The development of a double heart like hers is my prayer for you (and for myself). It is essential for sanctity, and I'm sure it is a good description of Mary's heart. Remember that God suffers for us and with us. The human and divine response to the faults of the

[5] Simone Troisi and Cristiana Paccini, *Chiara Corbella Petrillo: A Witness to Joy*, trans. Charlotte J. Fasi (Bedford, N.H.: Sophia Institute Press, 2015), p. 159.

world is a cry, and he wants us to unite our sufferings to Christ for the saving of mankind (Col 1:24)—to share in his pain and in his glory. Give your pure pains to God, because they are an echo of Christ's pain, a protest against injustice and cruelty. You are not alone. Never think, in whatever grief you may find yourself, that you are alone. The story of humanity is written in the life of Jesus Christ. Everything that happens to you can be found in him, and in the life of his Mother.

"There is no such thing as a hierarchy of grief," an old lady once said. Her parents had been killed in the Nazi death camps, and she was scolding another old lady whose parents had also been killed in the Holocaust. They were sitting in a group of psychiatric patients, and talk of suffering had become quite competitive. How could the old Irish lady, who was simply depressed, compete? "Sadness is sadness," the first lady would say.

The shape of sadness is universal: Christ represents it in his affliction and shouldering of the world's sin and pain, and though there is large grief and small, the lady was not wrong. Each of your pains, however seemingly inconsequential to others, is part of a fractal pattern with Christ's pain; you suffer in him, he suffers in you and with you. In prayer, your pains are raised from your shoulders. They rise to God and say: *The world needs to be closer to you.*

∽

I will tell you something: I am tired of being afraid. I am sorely tired of being afraid.

I am tired of worrying about terrorist attacks and which part of me might get cancer. I am bored with fretting about the future and whether we will have enough money. I am burned out with anxiety about plastic use and carcinogens and how I can avoid them. I have no more energy left to worry about whether you have done your homework or whether you will ever start studying in earnest.

At this point in your life as I write, before we put the light out you will sometimes be gripped by a worry that you have to share with me. "Now is not the time," I say. The dark, like water on wine, expands worries until there's a flood and no one sleeps. "Wait till we can think clearly in the daylight." So I snuff out your concerns, about an assignment or a dental appointment, as best I can, and then I turn out the light.

Be careful, I said to you one evening, not to acquire a habit of worry. We, as a family, have a tendency to *need* a worry in our heads. Without it we feel empty, even panic-stricken, as though we must have forgotten something vital. This habit of worrying, like a way of walking or a laugh, has been passed down for generations. Some have succumbed more than others. Your great-grandmother was always animated by anxiety: would the house catch fire, would she make a fool of herself at the parish meeting, what would the vicar think if he came round and saw Granddad tapping out his pipe in the kitchen sink? Misery can inhabit us in the same way.

Your great-great-aunt was horrified to discover the facts of life on her wedding night, and she never got over it. When she had a baby, the child died tragically after a few weeks, and she had no more children. Her beloved husband died when I was a child. When I visited her years later, she was in her eighties and still bent to the shape of her sorrows. The repetition of her sad stories was a groove from which she could not break free. They had come to define her, and the scar tissue that held their shape was bitterness and blame —particularly directed towards my grandmother, who was a nurse and should, my great-aunt felt, have saved the baby; who was a big sister and should have taught her siblings the facts of life.

My great-aunt had written a memoir of accusation, and the thick manuscript sat on the table between us like a loaded gun. Through the grey window, London disappeared. It seemed as if my great-aunt had harnessed time. She had attempted to freeze her pain in its moments of explosion—when the pieces of grief fly up and out and the bereaved might ask why or even wonder what happened; when anger and bargaining are ways of juggling what has occurred to keep it from falling, unnegotiable, to the ground. For when the pieces of a death have fallen into place and the reality has, eventually, been accepted, the bereaved have to carry their grief for a lifetime, often unnoticed. It becomes something no one would guess that they suffer; people can even forget about the person who died (this can be the hardest thing of all). My great-aunt grasped her misery and proffered it to anyone who would listen. Sixty years on, she was still wrangling over the details of her wedding night and her lost baby, as well as the death of her husband and the actions of her dubious relatives. She was holding on to her gross misfortune as though it were the one thing left to her.

If only she had known that she did not need to hold on so tightly. Surely nothing is worse than the loss of a child, and the overwhelming temptation must be to remain in the place and the moment of his life and death. But if we can wrench our grief from the depths and hand it over to God, then in all those dark and unexplored spaces where we are ripped apart, he will surely pour himself.

In any grief, our great challenge is to yield to chronological time, with its power to move pain on and eventually to diminish it—or at least to change its shape (and we shouldn't underestimate the usefulness of psychological help in achieving this; God works through men too).

This surrendering to chronological time is easier if we can also place ourselves in liturgical time, which is in fact timeless and renders every moment present. So we are not abandoning the lost child; we are not forsaking noble and natural suffering. God keeps it all for us. Remember that Christ's wounds are always fresh. They retain the necessary impact of his violation—

that is why the divine sacrifice of the Mass is as good today as it was the day that he was crucified.

My poor great-aunt was not unusual in the way she held on to her misery; it is a very common trait, to greater and lesser degrees, in all of us. But if she could have placed her wounds in Christ's, she might then have been better able to let go of the fear of her grief becoming dusty or forgotten (or of the "culprits" not being brought to justice). When we give our wounds to him, bitterness and resentment are washed away, leaving them healthy and brimful of the love that is inseparable from any grief. This love has the power to turn the most awful suffering into redemption because it unites us with Christ (whose wounds express love itself).

When Jesus appeared to Saint Faustina, a Polish nun, he told her there was one more thing she had to give him. She was confused. She had given him everything: her love, her obedience, even her will. No, he said, there was one more thing that she was holding on to tightly, the one thing that belonged entirely to her: her misery. She saw that it was true, and later she wrote, "A ray of light illumined my soul, and I saw the whole abyss of my misery. In that same moment I nestled close to the Most Sacred Heart of Jesus."[6]

"Do not be afraid," the angel Gabriel said, and his words resounded from that afternoon through the

---

[6] *Diary of Saint Maria Faustina Kowalska: Divine Mercy in My Soul* (Stockbridge, Mass.: Marian Press, 2006), no. 1318.

whole of Mary's life, and to everyone called to respond to God's proposal in every moment. It is often our misery that stops us from letting God in to the *now*. It stops us from seeing its color, its value, its way of bringing us closer to him.

I get the impression that you think that if you relax your white-knuckle grip on your worries, you will fall from some tree and never stop falling. It isn't true. In the spaces that would breathe through your fingers and mind, God himself would flood and show you that you do not need to be afraid.

Here, then, is another good reason to pray: hand God your misery so it doesn't impede you and define you. *Give it up*. You will make space for him to dwell in you. Here is another good reason to go to Mass: it is our glimpse of God's time, of eternity, where all, past, present, and future, are held. Your pains are united to Christ's sacrifice and transformed for our redemption. Your plans (even if they seem to fail) and hopes are made good in him. You will lose nothing. Relax your hands. Pray. Put out the light.

Sleep.

3

Behold, I am the handmaid
of the Lord (Luke 1:38)

Who am I?

This is the question that has plagued you most. And not just you. It has become the question of your generation. *Who am I?* Who am I if I can't get good grades, and five hundred likes on social media, and have my own YouTube channel? Who am I if I don't earn much, don't have a husband; if I'm married but have no children? If I have no job but stay home to look after my kids? Who am I if I'm divorced and on my own, if my company collapses, if I have few or no friends? Who am I?

"Behold," Mary said—which is one way of telling someone you're very sure of who you are—"I am the handmaid of the Lord."

From the empty dawn of before all time, Mary's life was also headed to that question *Who am I?* and to that answer, "Behold . . ." For her, the path to the answer was likely straighter, but the challenges steeper. For the rest of us, it is a question that detains us, that we fret over and change our minds about; it can throw us off course, further away from our true selves. It can make us feel uncertain, inadequate. It can make us feel lonely, make us take a lot of lovers, make us have plastic surgery, make us think we're not, or shouldn't be, what we plainly are (a boy or a girl, flat chested or buxom, a mother or someone destined to be childless).

My love, who are you?

To begin with, you were a beautiful baby. In a poem, I described your full, sleeping face as a peony about to bud. Your skin glowed an Italian olive but at the same time had an English porcelain delicacy. From the start, your default reaction was mirth, and when you laughed, your dark eyes crackled with light. In your first years your limbs were soft and springy as thick moss. I dressed you in palest pink chiffon for your baptism. I didn't believe, then, in God or baptisms, but I believed in parties and nice frocks and in having some class.

When the priest carried you through the grey stone church at the end of the rite, his words jarred in my head. They were words that seemed contrary and plain wrong. He had washed you of Original Sin, he said; *now* you were pure. And I thought, *Bilge.* You were the one pure thing in that church. You were the cut pink rose that was, still, spotless.

I intuited that as time went on that would change— our handling of you, the world's interference, would damage you, incrementally. We as your parents were damaged goods, and our anxiety, our wounds, our incompetence and clumsy love would bruise you. And when I weaned you from the breast I felt that you would be mottled, too, by what came in physically from the outside. Your body would begin to absorb the chemical pollutants of how we have chosen to create food, just as your mind would absorb the pollutants of words, and your spirit the warped heredity of human love.

Of course, as you grew, the imperfections did emerge, just as they emerge in everyone, even the greatest saints. You had fears that failed to be calmed. There were wounds in your self-esteem, some caused by people, some that budded from deep inside you, echoes of old wounds from your parents, your grandparents, your great-grandparents. As with any child, the first disobedience came, the first lie. And your good qualities—your loyalty, your sensitivity, your imagination —sometimes seemed like obstacles to fitting in with the fast-paced fun of your school friends (for if there is one thing that you are, it is a thinker, and you have always needed time alone and quiet).

You were very English for a child born and raised near Rome to an Italian father. You would only whisper a word, after a long pause, to a stranger. You bemused the nursery staff with your exquisite table manners. We had to tell the primary teacher that if you said you were unwell, *you were unwell*. You were not given to Italian hyperbole. But in time, the Italian Flo emerged too, and she was sassier, feistier. She told me off and swore at her father. She was interested in getting to know the system only so that she could figure out how to beat it. I found it hard to take her seriously.

Like everyone else, you became a chaos of traits and flaws, talents and kindnesses, some inherited, some just you, some from the culture, some deliberately taken on to fit in.

As you grew, some of your friends dyed their hair and took to wearing fake glasses to school to give themselves an intellectual air (I struggled to explain why this latter was wrong). You, like your friends, slid into doctoring photos of yourself on your phone, and I attempted to explain when this was OK (bunny rabbit ears) and when not (making your eyes bigger or your neck longer). I was up against a tide. We were part of a larger culture that told us it was OK to have plastic surgery, or even to choose our gender and undergo surgery to achieve it. Notwithstanding the small percentage of people born with chromosomal confusion or congenital disorders, these boys who think they are girls, and vice versa, are desperately asking this same question: Who am I? These people, who are building their own identity from made-up language and stitches and scalpels, are thrashing around for something to grip.

They are like my friend Wendy from Camden, who went from being a quiet musician with few friends to someone who maintains that she is neither male nor female and answers only to "they". Her clothes are meant to be "gender neutral" and so is her hair, but she looks like a convict who has had hope sucked out of her by a Soviet-style system, someone who has had the Divine Artist's finest brushstrokes erased. She has shaved her eyebrows, and she cuts her legs with a razor. Instead of heralding a brave choice and personal happiness, she, like Crow, is a desperate symbol of rejection. She has rejected (tragically, unwittingly; one could say with diminished free will) God's call for her: who she *is*.

Who am I? we wonder, desperately, as we grow.

Mary, as we know, was disturbed by the angel's greeting: "Hail, full of grace, the Lord is with you" (Lk 1:28).

Why would she be so perturbed? In the original Greek, "hail" is an ordinary salutation—which, by no accident, also happens to mean "rejoice". But in fact, Gabriel does not follow this greeting with "Mary". The word he uses to address her is a very unusual word, and he uses it instead of her name. It would be like calling her "Full-of-Grace" or "Favored One".

All the way through Scripture God gives new names. Abram becomes Abraham; Jacob becomes Israel; Simon becomes Peter. In doing this he is signing what people *are* and what they are called to do. Although Mary never loses her given name, the angel's use of another word to greet her reveals to her, just for a moment, how God sees her: what she *is*.

The naming of things has always been a sacred matter. Think about Eden. God created, but he brought each thing to man, for *man* to name (Gen 2:19). This image is powerful. It is as if Adam stepped around a dim garden, lighting each bird and animal with one precisely chosen word, and by naming it he owned it and knew it better. What a gift of creation! In Judaism a name has great significance; it captures the essence of a person: you know a person when you know his name.

Furthermore, in Hebrew, the word "to know" is related to intimacy. There is deep sense in this. If we truly *know* a person (his core, his thoughts, his history), it seems to me that we are better able to truly *love* him. That is why God loves more and better than anyone else—because only he completely and inexhaustibly *knows*.

He knows every shift, permanence, swell of love, light, and darkness in your heart. He knows what precedes your thoughts and actions, what follows them, and exactly how much free will you have in any given moment. This divine knowledge is the root of his mercy. This is why, of all persons, you have the least to fear from him.

God knows us, he knows our true name and what we are called to be (Rev 2:17). It seems to me that this is why Mary was so startled at the angel's words. It was the amazement of recognition.

Mary had always walked in God's gaze, but the Annunciation brought this to a new consciousness. She lifted her head like someone who is called aloud after a lifetime of prayerful silence. She heard her name, a name that contained the significance of not necessarily how she viewed herself or her state that day but her truest self, which always contains God's plan for us. And though, in her most profound modesty, she could hardly have guessed at the magnitude of what that might mean, she of all people would have recognized the rightness of God's vision of her. Full of grace. One who will be filled with God. Who will be nearest to God.

Mary is without sin. She is the cut pink rose that never browns at the edges of its petals. She has not inherited the twisted, gnarled growths of sin through her being that the rest of us have. It did not take much to make her realize *herself* in God's gaze—just that moment of soft rupture, that moment of being "troubled".

For you and me, this realization of ourselves is more difficult. Anxiety makes us illogical, and deaf to God's gentle call. Stress can make us bad tempered, and bad judges of our own actions. But what shocked me about finding God (and this often happens in the minutes after Communion) was the realization of *myself* as I was gathered in his gaze.

After Communion, when Christ is in the physical depths of you, it is as though a lamp has been placed in the darkness of your soul where you truly *are*, where your secrets bud and your shame grows rank, where your dreams strain at the constraints of possibility. This lamp that is Christ throws light onto everything, and the light is painless; it even washes clean.

You may be aware of God watching you, just as he watched Mary. He sees far beyond the present moment to things you cannot know—and the contrarieties inside you, the scuffed days or moments that you would rather blot out, the things that make no sense and that you would never post on social media. He knows all of that, and deeper, further; and in the context of that knowledge, pain and shame are lost.

In those moments of prayer, the light of his gaze will give you coherence and some understanding of the person you really are. This sense of yourself is far from the modern notion of discovering your "identity". It is a glimpse into the mystery of your soul in creation. It is like looking from a hilltop down onto a town and understanding how the twisted streets and accidents of history and planning make a shape. It is knowing that God *knows*.

Mary heard God's name for her that afternoon, and then she heard his incredible divine plan. And then she could say, "Behold, I am the handmaid of the Lord." She knew that the authenticity of her *self* lay in doing God's will. He made her; he loves her; he knows her. His plan for you, like his plan for her, will, as Saint Catherine of Siena wrote, set the whole of Italy and the world ablaze.[1] Only in fulfilling God's plan for ourselves will we find peace. But first we must listen to God and recognize *who* we are.

∼

[1] Letter of Catherine of Siena to Stefano Maconi.

The problem is that being who you are doesn't always feel comfortable, does it?

You've always been painfully aware of having an English mother. By the age of four or five, you already knew that being foreign is a mortification worthy of the most intrepid saints. There is something damaging to the soul in not being understood. This condition is the antithesis, after all, of how we are in God: completely known and comprehensible. When you are away from home, living with a language that is not your own, this becomes a continual friction, sackcloth against the skin, a stone in the shoe.

With this acquired language, you are not clever any more; you can't be funny (how many times did I tell a joke only to find the punch line was null and void in Italian?). No one understands your achievements or your history. You dress differently. You might offer a drink as soon as someone comes into your house, which in your country is polite but in this new country is seen as rude. Who you are (or who you have evolved to be in your culture) rubs painfully against the unfamiliar shape of this new place. I'm sorry you sensed that in me.

When I was pregnant with you I thought that from the day of your birth you would be more Italian than I could ever be. How wrong I was. At the age of ten, you were still known at school as the English Girl. The world that you were born into was my arms, my language, the way that I thought. The outside world, at least at first, was foreign.

It upset (and bewildered) me that you felt like an outsider too. I guess you picked up on my discomfort at the school gate when I could not get the jokes and when my concerns were not the concerns of the Italian mammas. "They don't want to talk to you," you once said, "because you're younger than they are." In fact, I was older, but you saw my cluelessness as an outsider and mistook it for youth. The truth was that the Italian parents did not know me or understand me. And, as we now know, this meant that they did not, or could not, love me.

I now believe that your feeling of being an outsider (and mine) is not because we are English in a foreign country (because you are also, now, thoroughly Italian). I believe it is God drawing us closer to him (and this is how suffering can also be a gift). By allowing us to feel like eternal outsiders, he is offering us a pass to be holy. He is making us realize where home really is.

One summer we decided, rather ambitiously, to build a grotto in the garden and place a statue of the Lourdes Madonna inside. We collected shells and broken pieces of crockery to brighten the turf and tried to half bury an upturned plastic doll's bath. It didn't work. In the end, we superglued the statue to the top of the back garden wall, where, in the rose-gold light of late afternoon, she seemed almost alive.

As I cooked and chatted with you, I liked seeing her through the window, framed by mastic leaves. It made me think of how she appeared to Bernadette Soubirous with yellow roses at her feet, speaking in Gascon Occitan. And how she appeared to Juan Diego in Mexico, speaking in Nahuatl. Our Mother is our homemaker; she understands the importance of the mother tongue and the sights that we are used to. But she also understands more than anyone the uselessness of belonging to a gang of girls, to a tribe, to a country, to this world. As our Mother, she asks us to find our home in her arms. Then she will walk us to our true home, Christ.

Our first language is not, after all, our mortal mother's. Our first language is the language of God, and these words, which we mostly know now as silence, we were listening to before our birth and will continue to hear after our death. In this life, we know this language as prayer.

Like Christ himself, like Mary, we are not of the world (Jn 17:14). The more you feel an outsider, the fewer likes and hearts you garner on your phone, the more you feel that visceral discomfort of being different, the more you are like Christ. Christ broke down the tribal barriers of Jew and Gentile. He went to the people on the margins—the Samaritan woman, the lepers, the sinners. He came to embrace the world. He jolted people out of their complacent attitudes of belonging. Because the truth is that we belong only to him. The people that you meet may not know it, but they came from the same common starting point as you, and they are made to be headed for the same destination.

Christ is your brother. God Almighty is your Father. He gave you a Mother (Jn 19:27). And the family of saints is vaster than even the extended families in Santa Marinella!

> Do you not realize that Jesus Christ is in you? (2 Cor 13:5)

If you will let yourself feel that you belong to God, others will see this. They will see the knowledge (love) in your eyes of living in two cultures, of understanding the misery of the guy from Libya washing windshields at the traffic lights, and the dizzying aloneness of the man from India selling painted shells on the street. Anyone, even the one who most fits in and is most connected, may turn to you in a difficult moment and see Christ, who cuts through to our common humanity, in you.

~

That afternoon, Mary knew who she was. She declared herself the "handmaid of the Lord", and in that she was giving herself to him not only for the fulfillment of his divine plan but also as a total gift of self. By calling herself a "servant" or a "slave" she was speaking within her own Hebrew tradition: "O LORD, I am your servant" (Ps 116:16).

How fully conscious Mary was in the moment that she was about to become not only the Mother God himself but of *all* the faithful, and that her Son would grow and refer to us as his brothers, sisters, and mothers (Mt 12:49–50) we cannot know. Who *she* is turns out to be important for who *you* are.

Remember one spring when you couldn't bear to go to Mass midweek (it happened to be Holy Thursday)? We were driving through town, I was trotting out the arguments: that it was the institution of the Eucharist, that it was your solemn duty to be there, that it would be fun to watch Padre John wash people's gnarled old feet. You were whining like a creaky gate and threatening me with total refusal. And then, as we drove along by the sea in the direction of home, I remembered again my first Holy Thursday as a Catholic.

It was one of those occasions when Christ's presence at the side altar was so palpable. I remember the church as dark, the silver box borne aloft, huge and unwieldy, the immense number of white lilies and chrysanthemums, and a tremendous pull to him. I can't tell you how far words or petitions were from my mind and heart. The Person I loved beyond and above all things (and you, even at four, understood that, and how my love for God raises up even higher my love for you) was alone in a dark garden in such a state of dread and fear that he sweat blood (*hematidrosis*: this phenomenon is no metaphor). "Could you not watch one hour?" he asked Peter (Mk 14:37). Like a sister, like a mother, I wanted to put my arms around him, to take, if I could, any part of his pain. I could not bear to leave him, and he seemed to draw me to him like a riptide.

God chooses to need us. Think about that. God has no actual need of anything. He is complete, perfect, and omnipotent. Furthermore, the Father could have given his Son the supernatural strength not to suffer in his

Passion. Instead, he sent a consoling angel. But Christ also asked for human solidarity. If Peter had kept vigil with him in his agony, he may have made a material difference to Christ that night. Jesus, despite his divinity, wanted that human presence. He needed Peter. He chooses to need me, and he chooses to need you. God is outside time, and all time is present through liturgy. Therefore, that night, we can comfort Christ in his terrible suffering by receiving him, then by staying close to him. We can cradle him, in the form of the Eucharist, within ourselves.

I nursed many patients long ago who had poor sight and hearing; often their memory was bad. When I offered my hand it was usually taken hungrily, and held tightly. Think about it: this hand arrived from out of nowhere, and I was no one to them. My skin wasn't familiar, as a daughter's would be. But I never had the gesture rejected. And the hand that I held revealed so much about that person: his strength, his level of anxiety, his need for physical contact.

Yet I still didn't appreciate the power of touch until I gave birth (my first real experience of pain) and, after that, when I experienced dry socket syndrome after dental extractions (you will remember this; you put me to bed and brought me your toy dog). Pain, like love, can blot out the world. It stampedes through anything reasonable or harmonious. My pain, though smaller than Christ's, made me think nonetheless about the driving of a nail through a wrist—how it would require a demonic disregard of the form of carpal bones and tendons. The roar of pain and senselessness would be deafening.

My own lesser pain went on so long that I had to try to find a way of living with it. I took to thinking of it as a piece of bright jewelry I had with me always and must bear despite its agony in my flesh. I had to divorce it from talking to you because you didn't deserve my ill humor (chronic pain makes us irritable).

When I returned to the dentist's chair for him to scrape the bone and restart the healing process, the staff said to me, "Why are you crying?" All their attention was on my wrenched-open mouth. And then a nurse gently stroked my cheek with the knuckle of her index finger. The effect was disproportionate to the act. It was as though I were sheltered for some moments out of violent wind. It carried with it a sudden stillness and the overwhelming surprise of kindness and understanding.

There is even a scientific theory to explain this: the gate control theory of pain. This says that when we are hurting, a sense of touch on the sore place can block pain messages and prioritize the sensation of benevolent touch in the brain. My pain was too great to be totally annulled by the nurse's caress, but her action flooded me with calm.

Touch offsets not just physical pain—which explains why my hand was held so hungrily by those elderly people. It makes me think of Veronica's seemingly infinitesimal gesture in wiping the face of Christ on the road to Calvary.

Veronica's touch must have been a chord of harmony and sanity at a demonic scene. It's important to remember that "good" (which includes kindness) is "right"; it is what we were made for. We recognize it in chaos as the sheep recognizes the voice of the shepherd. The gate control theory could be seen as metaphysical too: God gives greater value to our better selves (which is why there is no sin too large to forgive as long as we are truly sorry). Veronica's act must have sung with perfect pitch among the evil cacophony. No wonder Jesus left her the imprint of his face.

The Eucharist is the meeting of your flesh with Christ's, and taken in the right state, his Heart can be touched and consoled. We can give him that moment of harmony and rightness. We can embrace him as he embraces us.

This, then, is also who you are: someone whom God has chosen to need. Your love for him is not futile. Your prayers—particularly those of simply loving him—repair the bond between God and man; they strengthen the bond between God and you; they work against sin and its effects and pour grace into the world. But this isn't why we pray like that, necessarily. You can't fake praying like that. You pray like that simply because you love.

So, as I drove you home, I talked about the dark garden of Gethsemane and his dread, and being alone, and, of course, you understood. And so you said with sober sincerity, "Yes, I'll come."

Years later you told me, "But I don't love Christ like you do." Yet I knew that the kernel of love was in you, because it is a part of your empathy and your humanity. And the remedy for not being able to feel that love is to allow God to love you—that is, to sit before him and to quiet the voices of the world that define you by grades, what it is you "do", how rich you are, how many friends you have. To listen and know that he suffered and died for you. *You* no less than any of the other billions he died for. Particularly you. For God is infinitely large and infinitely small. He is universal and particular.

These days, when you complain about the one girl in the class who gets straight As and does ballet or tennis or swimming every day, and you compare yourself to her, I tell you to remember that God has a plan for you that neither she nor anyone else can fulfill. In Christ you will be as he intended you to be and do things that no one else can do. Your self-realization may be quiet; it may not garner awards and money. But done for God it will bring you peace and happiness beyond anything you could imagine. You need only relax, stop questioning, just for a while, and say with Mary, "Behold, I am the handmaid of the Lord."

4

Let it be to me according to your word (Luke 1:38)

Becoming a mother is always a tremendous thing. "Let it be with me"; "Let it be done to me"; "Avvenga per me"; "Qu'il me soit fait"; "Γένοιτό μοι." Whichever translation, whichever language we hear it in, these words are inextricable from the moment a woman discovers she is carrying a child, an "other", *someone else*. And the heavens hold their breath to hear her *fiat*. Of course, God's will does not always involve something as large as a pregnancy—and you may have one child, many children, or none. But as we're thinking about the Annunciation, pregnancy seems a good place to begin.

I discovered your existence on our last day in Sardinia. We were packing up the flat in a hurry to leave for Rome, and the knowledge that you had come into being blasted any other thought from my skull. By the time we boarded the boat at Olbia, I felt the beginning of a nausea that seemed very much like fear. I had been so anxious to leave the island and so worried about your father's job that I'd had difficulty swallowing food, and our doctor prescribed a drug that might help. It would have no negative consequences on any pregnancy, she reassured me when I told her that we were trying to have a baby. Still, I had doubts about the medicine—I took it only once, on a bad day. Now, though, boarding a ship with you in my womb, I remembered that pill and knew its ingestion would have coincided with your earliest days. Since doing the pregnancy test, I'd looked the drug up online: it was a pill that could cause a harelip in children whose mothers took it in the first trimester of pregnancy.

The darkness of the port and the ship's bright, swaying corridors were nightmarish. I could not believe what I had done: I had damaged something infinitely precious before it had even begun. When I called a friend in dry-mouthed panic, she finally suggested I have an abortion. "Why don't you begin again with a clean slate?" they said. I was not against abortion then. At least it was something that I gave little thought to, and you would certainly have been defined in my mind as the "cluster of cells" abortionists speak of.

I coldly considered this "getting rid of you" and "beginning again". It was a very modern solution, even logical. But nothing within me could consent to it. I did not know you then, but I had the insight that no pregnancy would be perfect—that nothing was perfect. I might not even be able to get pregnant again. No, I couldn't throw away this child because of uncertainty. But I thought, with anger, of the lovely doctor who had taken such good care of me, and I wondered why she had been so adamant that the pill could not harm a pregnancy. She was not stupid or malign. I had no more access to internet on the boat. I was adrift on a black sea with you inside me and your father asleep next to me and no God to pray to. The strangest word presented itself in my head: "Trust."

As an atheist, it was a word I was totally unfamiliar with. The thought of placing my trust in the doctor loomed above me, and I felt a certain lightness. I saw that I could not bear this, any of this, alone and that I had no control over what was happening to me. It was a fleeting sensation, but it was a foretaste of the trust I would later put in God.

Needless to say, my calm did not last. Once ensconced in our new house I hooked up to the internet and became a crazed expert on early embryonic development. The more I learned, the more comforted I would feel, only to feel panic descend on me again and the frenzied need to find one piece of incontrovertible evidence that I had done you no harm.

The spiral ended only when I contacted a doctor friend in London who told me that one pill of anything, these days, is unlikely to do any damage, and there was barely a woman alive who didn't regret something she had done in the early days of pregnancy— a pill, a drink, a *lot* of drinks. "Welcome," my Jewish doctor friend told me, "to the guilt of motherhood. It begins now, and it never ends."

Her words were the beginning of my *fiat*: my formal consent, which was really an atheistic acknowledgment of my powerlessness (an important step in conversion); an acceptance of chaos and imperfection with its inherent call to suffering; a letting go and a step out into darkness. I had no guarantee as to how you would be, and yet I began to fall in love with you. And when I first felt the quickening of you within me, I began to know something of you and therefore to lose my heart completely. You see how important flesh can be?

My creaky trust was the vaguest echo of the trust that Mary would have had in God from the very beginning. How weighty that trust must have been for her to say, "Let it be to me according to your word!"

"Wait," another person might say, "could I have a day or two to think this through?" Remember: as a betrothed woman at that time, pregnant before married to her husband, she was terribly vulnerable. Yet she gives an embracing consent that is even more akin to someone stepping out into darkness with no clue as to where her feet will fall. Yet her eyes are not blinded; they are fixed steadily on God. Mary is exceptionally courageous. But it is courage built on trust in God, not recklessness.

In the face of incalculable uncertainty, she could know only that she had something unique and unfathomable within her womb. How much more awesome for her, then, would Christ's quickening have been—disarmingly normal, but at the same time the first conscious physical touch between man and God: a presage of the Eucharist. (Remember this when you receive Communion: Mary was the first to know Christ physically in the dark of her body.)

You see, when we feel incredulous about biblical events, we have to remember the incredible grace in ordinary lives. If, as an atheist, I felt my fear melt in the face of your emerging life, it does not seem so very remarkable that Mary—who faced such daunting unpredictability—sang for joy by the time she met Elizabeth, even though it was long before her own quickening. She had God; she had knowledge through love of God; through God she *knew* the child within her. What happened to her was not ordinary, but it was a transformation of a very ordinary human story. And, thanks to her, we have echoes of the extraordinary (her courage, her faith) to strive for in each of our own human situations.

But every mother, it seems to me, fears exception, and though I do not doubt Mary's joy (and thank God for Saint Joseph's protection of her), we know she was not spared natural pain and anxiety (Lk 2:48). This was a real family, not the stuff of legend, and difference in any child tends to difficulty. Every mother with a child who is exceptional, whether because of a stammer, a disability, or a gift, can look to Mary and know that she understands. And every such child can claim a privileged brotherhood with Christ. We know so little of his childhood, and we're educated with pious notions of a cozy and holy home. They may well be accurate enough. But a mantle of difference and danger hung over them from the very beginning, and Mary, like any mother, suffered, and suffered more.

"Let it be to me according to your word." Did she know, that afternoon, what she was surrendering to? Did she foresee his quiet yet revolutionary mission and his bloody death?

What I want to stress is that suffering without God is tangibly different from suffering with him. God gathers up our despair, our wretchedness and fear, and works for good (Rom 8:28). He is like a father picking up the pieces of shattered crockery that a child has hurled onto the kitchen floor, and crafting them into something else, maybe something even better. Remember the young Sardinian priest; remember Chiara Corbella. Remember, if or when you do find that you are to become a mother, that you must not be afraid.

What pregnancy illustrates is that accepting God's will (in whichever form it takes—religious life, childlessness, motherhood, mission) always means birthing a beauty *beyond ourselves*. We may not be able to grasp it—we may look at the crying child in our arms and just wish she would sleep—but we must trust that the loving acceptance of his will redeems us. Under the cross, Mary suffered a passion of motherhood that is indescribable. But in those hours she birthed the Church, and she continues to do so (Rev 12:2). Her pains bring man and God closer. In a smaller sense, so will your pains, if they are your work for God's will.

This is the work of every vocation: to diminish the distance between man and God.

We pray regularly for you to discover your vocation. But a vocation is not a coat you put on like a doctor. There is no vocation from which you can "clock out". A vocation is something we surrender to moment by moment. Of course, this may express itself in a great theme: a career, a mission, a large family. But I think, too, of the people we don't talk about: the old lady whose husband died who cooks for the parish priest and shops for her disabled neighbor. She suffers from chronic arthritis, but she never fails to smile and remember people's names. She, too, is living her vocation.

We're more susceptible than we realize to a Hollywood worldview. (How would my life look as a film? Where is its climax, its heroism, its catharsis?) Reality is messier. Sometimes God works through what a screenwriter would fail to serve up as a story. Your calling may present itself in different forms over time, even over different days or hours. But this fact does not change its central integrity: responding to God's unique proposal to you.

God will find you and let you know his plan for you, whatever it might be. The story of your earliest existence should show you that; he was already finding me in your first hours. Our lives were already long in his sights. He keeps vigil with us in our darkness. He makes use of our bleakness to show us that we need to trust. And, as Julian of Norwich says, "the Nature-goodness that we have of Him enableth us to receive the working of Mercy and Grace."[1] Even before we are saints, even before we are believers, God is there, and when our soul is predisposed, he will speak to us, even in retrospect, even on that dark night in the boat, even when I spoke to my Jewish doctor friend. It is as though he spoke, and only years later did I know who was speaking.

But yes, there are things you can do to hear God's plan, to know it, and to consent to it, to make your path a little straighter—for yes, there can be casualties along the way. Some mothers are called to be far more courageous than I have, so far, been called to be. Children *are* aborted. Let's minimize these casualties. Let's cling to him.

~

In the fourteenth century Julian of Norwich experienced a rich "showing" of Christ, a vision, among fifteen other such revelations:

> And then our Lord opened my spiritual eye and shewed me my soul in midst of my heart. I saw the Soul so large as it were an endless world, and as it were a blissful kingdom. And by the conditions that I

[1] See chap. 57 in *Revelations of Divine Love Recorded by Julian, Anchoress at Norwich*, trans. Grace Warrack, Project Gutenberg EBook, September 2, 2016.

saw therein I understood that it is a worshipful City. In the midst of that City sitteth our Lord Jesus, God and Man, a fair Person of large stature. . . . The place that Jesus taketh in *our Soul* He shall never remove it, without end, as to my sight: for in us is His *homliest* home and His *endless* dwelling.[2]

Like all authentic mystical experiences, the message is true for Mary and it is true for you. That afternoon of the Annunciation, Mary was ready to submit herself to God's word in the most literal fashion. But she already had the city of God inside her soul, inside her heart, with Christ at its core. God's word was always a part of Mary, and so was Christ.

She prayed; she read the Scriptures. She knew of God's covenant with Israel, how he saved her people from slavery (Lk 1:54); she would have been familiar with his promise of a Messiah. There was nothing in her that doubted, fought against him, or made her think that she knew better. The city of God was within her. By this I mean that her soul was structured around faith, prayer, God's law and his presence. We talk about journeying towards the kingdom of heaven, but to reach it we need to cultivate its essence within ourselves.

When an infant learns a language, there is an awakening of certain parts of the brain; a structure is formed. Your brain houses two languages, and you are wired

[2] Ibid., chap. 67.

to speak them both effortlessly. The language of God is another structure that we are born with in our soul and that we must also activate and nourish. Mary had God's living word within her. The angel's words were startling, but they lit further an already existing lamp-stand in her soul.

For us, listening to God's word can be trickier. We are not immaculate. We live in a culture that many times goes against what he would have us do, that provides endless distraction and confusion. To counter this, we must pay attention to the city of God within ourselves and light all of its lights. To begin this, we need silence.

The absence of noise is truly a vanishing thing. It is barely possible to escape the sound of traffic, even in the middle of the countryside. I see you, like so many of your generation, incessantly turning to screens. Notifications ping. Even some restaurants have giant screens that pull us away from our companions and our meal.

Like me, you cannot bear too much noise and too many lights. "It makes everything abstract," you took to saying when you were ten. You are right: artificial noise and lights distort reality and block prayer. The natural pace of the body is jolted; thoughts are blasted. Recollection is all but impossible in a roar of artifice. Prayer, after all, enhances true knowledge of self and God. When our eyes are fooled by lights and our ears are deafened, we see reality as a Picasso portrait, dislocated and impossible to gather.

But you are fortunate in having those summer nights in Sardinia, where the noise of one television is soon drowned in the silence of the mountains and the sky as we walk. The sea is lost to blackness, and the silver olive trees are almost invisible. As we amble on, there is one square of dim light from the house, but no more, because light attracts mosquitoes, and your grandmother is still getting used to having electricity at home. The small dog runs ahead of us. The sheep's bells clank. When you look up, there are more stars than you can imagine. They are like ground-up salt crystals, tiny and glittering. There are so many, and with such a radiant light they look as though they have been smudged across the black by a giant thumb. Here we can witness the immensity of distance and the depth of silence. No one can reach you.

In a pressing emptiness such as this, you *might* find a taste of God. You might hear the "still small voice" of his presence (1 Kings 19:12). In silence like this, unimportant thoughts will die, and the mind is opened up to prayer. In silence you will know your smallness and your aloneness—and the impossibility of being alone, because God's presence is insistent in silence. Christ himself retreated into the wilderness and to the tops of mountains to pray. We cannot underestimate the importance of emptying our hands and minds and giving God all of our attention.

Yes, solitude and silence are important—but the construction of the city of God within you requires more. Many people will sense God in sunsets and oceans and forests. Gleaning *something*, they may turn to crystals, witchcraft, or Buddhism. They may take a gulp of nature and think, "That's just what I needed." What they lack, but what you will have through prayer and participating in the Holy Mass, is God's word. You cannot look at that vast black Sardinian sky and make any sense of its depth and its distances if you do not have this rooted within you.

Thankfully, learning God's word is not entirely about sitting in your catechism class and drily reading Scripture. For you, education has been all about tests and rote learning and more tests. I see a world of facts being flung like confetti all around you, and your hopelessness in letting them fall, uninterpreted, at your feet. No one explained to you why Mass mattered. Or even why equations mattered. No one cared about what you wanted to read or that Wednesday was dark blue and the number seven red. No one made the Mycenaeans seem any more than men in profile painted on ancient vases. No one was interested in finding that hunger in you that powers us through life.

"Where's the end of the sky?" you would say in the mornings when the silver of sea and sky were a seamless silk; "Why is that man out at sea so early?" as we drove past a boat silhouetted against the cold blue. Was it so hard, I would think, to inspire you with history and geography and the intricate music of mathematics? The problem is that formal education often lacks context.

God's word is the context for everything that you learn, and everything that you learn should be in context: a part of the ladder of being from single-cell creatures right through to human beings and angels. We should know how hierarchical structures exist right through nature, and heavenly creation too—how because of all *that*, the Church in turn is hierarchical. How patterns of plants and creatures are replicated in us (the daisy closes, just like your eyes, at night). How music can, however partially, express the Passion of Christ, and so by listening to Bach through my twenties I already, unwittingly, knew something of my Savior. How, through thermal radiation, a hand takes on the heat of a flame the closer it moves to it, and likewise the closer we move to God the more our bliss intensifies. How oranges are abundant when we're all at risk of coming down with colds, and how the dock leaf plant, with its antihistamine, grows close to stinging nettles. How, when you were given a piece of cloth that Saint Bernadette had touched, you murmured reverently: "Her DNA."

Everything, at root, is connected; science exists within religion. Mathematics is the scaffolding of music. Plants are the crude materials of medicine. The creation of a poem echoes the creation of the universe. It was meant to be that way.

And Scripture expresses what we are; Church teaching is about *us* at the truest and most intimate level. More than anything, learning God's word is like falling in love. Loving, remember, is knowing. A mother gets to know her child through her incomparable knowledge of his flesh, his smell, his voice. She sits beside him and listens to what he tells her, and absorbs it. In those first years, she will know best if he is in pain or distress and what he needs.

So it is with God and man. And the best place to sit with him and get to know him is in Adoration. This is like the vast Sardinian night sky, but with Christ in plain sight. Some people take a Bible along, or some kind of spiritual reading, but Adoration is not about too many words. It is about silently looking into the eyes of God. It is about becoming attuned to his gentle pushes and suggestions (and for us this is much easier to fathom here, with him, than it is outside in the vast wilderness). It is about taking one verse from Scripture and sitting with it, allowing God to unfold it for you. There is a rightness about sitting before the Blessed Sacrament—it is feeding ourselves with something absolutely right.

Psalm 1 tells us that men who study God's law are like trees (not lawyers or engineers). The teaching that they imbibe is not in units and PowerPoint presentations; it is like water, and this water brings forth fruit. People will tell you that God's teaching (they will say "Church teaching", "the Catechism", or "Catholicism") is hard. Some will say it's made up by men and is impossible to follow. They are missing the point. God's law is made up not of letters but of the Word in the form of Our Lord Jesus Christ. What this tells us is that God's law is written in human flesh and blood.

Scripture and the Catechism are to us what sheet music is to a symphony: they set down in ink the structure and the beauty of our nature as notes on a stave delineate and silently manifest sound. But the "sheet music" of Scripture and the Catechism was written in response to us—not to impose an unnatural code of conduct but to impart the knowledge of what we were made, most naturally and happily, to be.

You, as a baby in a pink bonnet being carried around the church after your baptism, were born with God's word branded on your heart; you were made for him. The shape of you was made to search for him, to desire him, to be satisfied, ultimately, only by him. The words that define you are the words of God, not the words of feminists, communists, fascists, nationalists, gender ideologues, or anyone else for that matter. The Word that breathed life into you set you on a course that is headed back towards the Word. But through your life there will certainly be other words that steer you, and none of them are neutral.

When I was a teenager I had no God. Aunty M and I were, like you, largely immune to the confetti of facts flung at us at school. Unlike you, we were not near any great metropolis or pieces of spectacular history. We were surrounded by desolate moor and grey granite. Our recreation was sitting on a low stone wall outside Saint Eustachius Church and talking our way out of our lives. We wore thick black eyeliner and long rain-coats bought from secondhand stores. Too soon we discovered the colorful softening and recklessness that alcohol brought into our world.

Without religion, books and music possessed a vital significance for us. We were not wrong in this—in fact, now when you find a book that enthralls you, I think, Yes! Lose yourself in it, find in it structures that are beautiful, people like you and unlike you, stories you wish you could live yourself. But perhaps even more than books and poems, music defined our days and became an almost liturgical crutch.

We discovered David Bowie by hearing *Hunky Dory* played through your uncle's bedroom wall. Soon, Aunty M and I would take the bus into Plymouth every Saturday to buy one old Bowie album at a time. We weren't disappointed: *The Man Who Sold the World*, *Ziggy Stardust*, *Aladdin Sane*—every single one was full of livid despair. Elegant, funny, cockney David was telling us, just us, that he understood: he too was a "Rock 'n' Roll Suicide". We listened to those songs as we dressed for school in the morning (tears streaking eyeliner), as we went to sleep; we sang them through lessons and lunchtimes. One song, "Quicksand", was explicit in its nihilism. There was no point at all in believing in yourself. True knowledge and peace would come only in death (a flagrant perversion of prayer). The song evoked the famous occultist Aleister Crowley, the nihilist philosopher Friedrich Nietzsche, and the creator of the Nazi death camps, Heinrich Himmler; the battle of light and dark.

These were our secular psalms. We repeated them. We turned to them. We took them as seriously and passionately as any cloistered nun takes her Office. They offered self-destruction as the only solution to life. Bowie himself had already emerged from cocaine addiction and into *Let's Dance* while we were descending into drinking heavily whenever we could, renouncing any hope of learning or getting qualifications, and hatching a half-baked scheme to run away to London and join a rock band (thank God that last never came to pass). It was all seen (at least the parts that the adults knew about) as a perfectly normal phase.

The fragility of the self in adolescence is a terrible thing. The comforts of childhood are no more; the power and certainty of adulthood are a long way off. Those who don't fit into the systems (the exams, the proms, the sports teams) flail around looking for something else to lean on. And there are plenty of possibilities: the occult, punk, drugs, and drink. Often the way that these alternative systems draw a person in are not so very different from the way that religions work: the renunciation of absolute control over your life (in religious terms we recognize that God is in charge; with alcohol and drugs, we are dabbling with disinhibition and stripping ourselves of responsibility), and seduction of the senses with words and music.

Words are powerful; never think they're not. The

gap between any word and what it describes is slender beyond measure—or it should be. (This is why it is so important to tell the truth. Lies attack our perception of the world.) People have always known the power of language, especially in repetition. In political propaganda and advertising, words are used to try to shape our understanding of a system or a product. If you expose yourself to the language of falsity and enough nihilism, like we did with the David Bowie songs, it will enter your bloodstream and distort rational thinking.

> Death and life are in the power of the tongue, and those who love it will eat its fruits. (Prov 18:21)

When I read about the Russian pilgrim searching for a way to pray without ceasing,[3] I was reminded of you when you were little and gamely reciting complicated prayers. The pilgrim meets an alcoholic man who has been given a copy of the Gospels in Old Slavonic, a language he doesn't read well. He is advised to read them anyway—because, as a monk tells him, even if he can't comprehend the Word of God, the demons certainly can, and they shake with fear.[4] What the pilgrim himself discovers is that speaking the Jesus Prayer aloud shapes his heart (we could also say his brain,

---

[3] *The Way of a Pilgrim*, a nineteenth-century Russian book by an unknown author, is wise and simple and will tell you what you need to know about the Jesus Prayer—one of the most powerful prayers in existence.

[4] *Way of a Pilgrim*, chap. 2.

thinking of neural pathways, but we are more truly talking about the seat of being, which is, traditionally, the heart). The words come to form his attention, his love, his understanding. Soon he is praying not just with his mouth but with his whole being, which is entirely alive and in harmony with what is being said—in brief, the essence of the Gospel: "Lord Jesus Christ [the Logos named, just as Adam named each creature to know them properly], Son of God [Peter's confession of who Jesus *is* (Mt 16:16)], have mercy on me a sinner [the tax collector's fundamentally correct and complete petition (Lk 18:13)]."

The name of Jesus Christ is the most powerful of all words in existence because it embodies God's law and love and the means of our salvation. Those who call on the name of the Lord will be saved (Rom 10:13), and we ask things in his name, as he told us to do (Jn 14:13). Whether you are walking, washing dishes, driving, or lying awake in the night besieged by thoughts, say the Jesus Prayer. The words will move through your body and shape your deepest thinking and your heart. This is another way that he abides in us and we in him (Jn 15:4). Language lives in us; it forms us. Let the words that you choose be the right ones, and you will become a tree planted beside a stream, absorbing Truth.

Pray the Psalms too. More than any pop song, they contain every facet of the human experience: longing, union, despair, exile, homesickness, and joy. The speakers of the Psalms are no strangers to darkness and the feeling of being an outcast. At the same time, the movement of the Psalms leads us up out of the pit (Ps 40:2) and into the courts of the Lord (Ps 116:19), where our heart's desire is fulfilled—from desolation to salvation and joy. The Psalms show us that every human emotion is housed in our longing for God. There is no depth to which you can descend where he will not reach you; there is no confusion or joy where he will not know you and meet you. The Psalms speak of perceived rejection: "O God, why do you cast us off for ever?" (Ps 74:1), and of the deepest truth: "God is the strength of my heart and my portion for ever" (Ps 73:26). They write the structure of the human psyche and allow you to walk through corridors of pain and abandonment while always leading you back to God.

> Some wandered in desert wastes,
> finding no way to a city to dwell in;
> hungry and thirsty,
> their soul fainted within them.

> Then they cried to the LORD in their trouble,
> and he delivered them from their distress;
> he led them by a straight way,
> till they reached a city to dwell in. (Ps 107:4–7)

I hear the songs that you listen to now, and they haven't changed so much from when I was young. There seems to be a strange pact between pop and nihilism. I have to stop myself from saying, "Don't listen to that!" when I hear one song glorifying being entirely alone until death (in a voice that's manipulated to sound childlike and does so, demonically). I end up blurting out, "You're not alone, not ever. You know that, don't you?" And I make you list Jesus Christ, our Blessed Mother, your guardian angel as persons all around your bed as you sleep. That existential aloneness of the void, the cigarette at 3 A.M., the dregs of whiskey, and seduction of hopeless songs is not your inheritance. Not anymore.

So this is one way you can prepare your heart to know your vocation: know and love God's word that is present in Scripture and in prayers. You will come to know dark songs and books. I imagine that you, too, will have your *Bell Jar* years—you'll read *The Outsider*, *Mrs Dalloway*, and the *Sorrows of Young Werther*. But what you will have, that I didn't have, is the city of God within you. Allow it to grow in you, street on street, dwelling on dwelling, so he can move smoothly through you in the Eucharist, lighting each light of your understanding and your calling at its proper time.

~

There are seven great lights in the city of God where you can meet Christ in privacy, as Nicodemus did: the sacraments. They are like lampposts on a road where suddenly there he is, waiting for you to stop for some minutes in clarity and shelter to talk with him.

You will have seen the sacraments ignored, even derided. We know many couples who live together but are not married. We know many unbaptized, many who don't go to Mass or confession.

We also know Elena, who divorced ten years ago and now shares her children's time with their dad. "Fifty percent of their lives," she whispered to me when this emerged at the divorce hearing. "I'll miss half my children's lives!"

Soon, the common routine of splitting time and home began. There was the bag that had to be carefully packed for the next three or four days. There was the aggression that came from one of the children for the first twenty-four hours of being back with Mom. There was the pain of the father's new girlfriend and the family outings that they planned, which Elena could not compete with.

All of this used to be described as a "broken home", and the children of such homes were observed for signs of disturbance. "Don't be too hard on him," my mother cautioned me once about a boy who was mean to me, "he's from a broken home."

But now these fractured families are so common they have become normal. Families "merge". Children have two moms, or two dads, and an assortment of step-siblings whom they see on a complicated schedule. Everything, Elena says, has become fractional: half-time mother, quarter-time stepbrother (who is also caught up in a rotating schedule with the family of his mother's new partner). No one is supposed to worry about it.

But Elena is a worrier.

Through the divorce and into the years afterward she

has been subjected to the usual "Have you met anyone?" Most people seem to find a new partner quickly.
Some go online to do so. Her divorced friends all dyed
their hair, upped their hemlines and their heels, and
were with someone new within the year. After three
years alone it looked like this wasn't going to happen
with Elena.

But she did draw closer to God. As she prayed, despite the fact that it was she who initiated the breakup
with her husband and could see no clear way to rec-
oncile with him, she felt the bonds of their marriage as
indissoluble. The pain, which presented itself as physical pains in her chest, came from the knowledge that
her husband was now with another woman, and her
children, for 50 percent of the time, were being moth-
ered by that woman. The pain was excruciating. But
no one understood Elena. The modern philosophy is
"Move on." And, even more, you *can't* remain alone.

Elena's aloneness intensified, and she was, more and
more, involved in a dance in the dark with God. There
were days on which he seemed so close that she felt
utterly consoled. There were days when the pain was
so bad and God seemed so distant that she collected
up all her icons and prayer cards and put them in a
cupboard—only to get them out again the next day.
Indisputably, these years alone have deepened her relationship with him: she is wrapped in his ineffable
presence on the couch in the evenings; she rises with
her coffee and the mysteries of the Rosary.

The surprise, for her and those around her who were

in attendance at her church wedding and knew that neither the bride (then) nor the groom was religious, is that she cannot escape the sacrament. The sacraments are the bones on which our stories take shape. They do not dissolve.

Elena has suffered so much, she has cried so much, she has had so many sleepless nights. Sometimes she asks—almost eleven years now since the divorce—why she continues to suffer. I think she loves God very much, and he loves her. She is experiencing a kind of mourning that Benedict XVI identifies as something ignited in us when we meet, nakedly, with truth. He relates this to the beatitude "Blessed are those who mourn, for they shall be comforted" (Mt 5:4).[5]

Elena's body knows God (she has the city of God within her), and that body is reacting to the state of her family and the society in which she finds herself. Christ's wounds are a consequence of our sin. They are God flinching at the cruelty of the world. Those who truly love God (like Elena) and therefore have some, albeit limited, knowledge of him will see, sometimes starkly and painfully, of course partially, the world as God sees it: "He who grows in love grows in grief."[6]

The fallout from endemic divorce is plain to see in the broken families around us: stress, financial ru-

[5] Benedict XVI, *Jesus of Nazareth: From the Baptism in the Jordan to the Transfiguration* (San Francisco: Ignatius Press, 2008), p. 86.

[6] Catherine of Siena, *The Dialogue of the Seraphic Virgin Catherine of Siena*, trans. Algar Thorold, chap. 1, "A Treatise of Divine Providence".

ination, confusion. The breakdown of the family sees children go undisciplined (because who wants to play the authoritarian parent on his two days of custody?), spoiled, or often shouldering responsibilities far beyond their years (I think of two little boys comforting their mother when it emerged that her new lover had a mistress, apart from the wife that she already knew about).

But society seems to have accepted this new wave of suffering as a price worth paying. In the morass of split families in the Western world that are somehow, supposedly, immune to this pain (or suppress it or sublimate it), I believe that Elena is bearing her agony in solidarity with Christ (Rom 8:17). She is reacting to the violence done to God's law: "What therefore God has joined together, let not man put asunder" (Mk 10:9). The personal pain that Elena feels is indicative of the wound that we as a society are inflicting on ourselves. If the sacraments are the scaffolding of the body of Christ—the bones of faith that help it keep its integrity and form—then we are breaking our own bones.

When Elena realizes the beautiful logic of her suffering, it brings her a sense of peace. After all, this type of sadness, as Benedict XVI goes on to say, brings the deepest conversion and hope, and I see this in Elena's face.[7]

~

[7] Benedict XVI, *Jesus of Nazareth*, p. 86.

We have already talked about how overwhelming human love can be. Perhaps, more than any other emotion, it can distort logic and reason, taking everything in its own direction like a forceful wind. It can contradict the sense of the whole world with its *rightness*. From experience, I can tell you that this can lead to mistakes. Listen: I doubt there's a person alive who hasn't sinned, who hasn't erred in relationships. Always pray. Never stop going to Mass (remember, you shouldn't receive Communion if you are in a state of mortal sin, *but God still wants you there*). Don't compound your sin by rejecting him when things get complicated—that would be the graver sin of pride.[8] Go to confession; you won't shock God. Nourish the city of God within you.

Always remember that your body is a temple of the Holy Spirit (1 Cor 6:19). This means that he guards you, he suffers in you and with you. I want to pass on a piece of advice given to me by your grandfather. He lived through the sexual revolution of the 1960s, though by 1965 he had married your grandmother and begun a family. "Don't give men what they want," he told me, and I sneered at what I saw as his old-fashioned naïveté.

"Why would I not want it too?" I pushed back.

"Women don't get it," he said. "They had this great bargaining tool, this enormous power, and they threw

---

[8] I heard this piece of advice from Julia Ashenden, whose father, the famous convert and priest Hugh Ross Williamson, told it to her when she was young.

it away. Most men don't want marriage particularly, but it used to be a way of being with a woman. Sex was the holy grail, and marriage was the way to get it. Then children came, and most men, once the kids arrive, are pleased. But it isn't often their idea in the first place. Now men can be with a woman anytime they want. Women blew it."

I thought he was silly. But I couldn't escape the fact that through my twenties none of the men I dated would talk about going on holiday together in the short term, let alone getting married and having children. The men I knew increasingly viewed the sexuality of a woman as separate from the woman. They wanted her medicated (on the pill), which was like unloading a gun for "safe play". They got bored of normal sexual contact and wanted things that had nothing to do with the woman as a person but only to do with frantically chasing a thrill that forever eluded them. That's what sex on tap, and pornography in particular, does to people: it leads them on to greater and greater extremes (that have nothing to do with love and sex and everything to do with debasement). Each new thrill doesn't satiate them for long. They are like hounds in a drag hunt being led by an artificial scent that will never satisfy them.

Your body is made to house God. You are not made to be a drag hunt for dogs after kicks. You know what love is through God's love for us all (Eph 5:25–33). The love of a truly loving man who wants the *whole* of you for all eternity will not look so very different.

The shape of love, like the shape of pain, is shared by man and God.

When you fall in love with the right person, you may get married. Your relationship with your husband will be a mirror of Christ's relationship with the Church (again, that fractal patterning, your life a visual echo of the divine); like all sacraments, it will bear witness to Christ's Passion and to the hope of our salvation.[9]

What can this mean? That your marriage carries the unchanging love of God, the pain of God, and our redemption through Jesus Christ within it. It will ask you to give yourself totally as Christ does; to be self-sacrificing, as Christ is; to be fruitful, as Christ is. It will not crumble if you both let God in. He will shelter and support your union. The sacraments will be your pillars and beams. When the deafening wind of passion dies down, you will be left with an enduring love, listening for that sheer silence of the Holy Spirit, who will speak to the parts of you that know about self-giving and caring for someone (even if that person has become ill, irascible, poor, or boring), about the stamina needed for eternity, and how you are carried by something far greater than that which the world tells you that you are: one woman.

You are a child of God, and your marriage is part of your salvation, and your husband's and children's, and even the world's. It is a far-reaching thing. Marriage

[9] See the apostolic exhortation *Familiaris Consortio* by Pope John Paul II.

is not easy. It can even be painful. There may even be exceptional circumstances in which it is better for a couple to live apart. But never think that there is not enough grace. That applies to every single situation you find yourself in, at every moment: *Never think that there is not enough grace.*

~

These days, when you feel lost, I try to explain that every moment of your life is an annunciation, though it may not be heralded by any visible angel, and you may be totally blind and deaf to its manifestation.

Nevertheless, God's will is announced to you in your waking, in each step you take to the kitchen, in what food you find on the table. It is in the starlings chattering under the eaves, in your obligation to go to school, and in your reluctant consent to do so. It is in the mist we breathe out on cold mornings, and in the three-car accident we pass on the road. It is in our parting kiss at the gate, even if we have quarreled on the journey. There is nothing we do that is not intimately connected with our Creator—what he wants, what he permits, what pains him, and what he may have chosen to intervene in, directly.

When I come into your room at night to tuck you in and you are curled up with a book, you always lay it down at the sight of me to unburden yourself from some preoccupation or to tell some hilarious story about your day. Together we place everything in God's hands, and when I trace the sign of the cross on your forehead, it is a physical smoothing out of your thoughts. The events of your life might not seem so big, even to you, when we think of Mary's encounter with the angel. But each moment is sent to us by God, and each moment has its own angel, your guardian angel, standing beside you to help you tackle it.

> Therefore do not be anxious about tomorrow. (Mt 6:34)

Take each moment like a fruit that will release its taste, its innate goodness. Be thankful for your bed, for the quiet night you have ahead of you. Know that the same angel will watch over you at school tomorrow. And in every moment—whether of fear, anxiety, or happiness —Christ is with you, the city of God is within you, and it is teaching you to act in imitation of him: to offer up your sorrows, to trust, and to be joyful.

Every moment contains God and his plan for you; Christ's wounds and their mercy for us; and Mary's unequivocal Yes. There is the *fiat* for our vocation—as a mother, a doctor, a writer, a missionary, or simply a very kind person who suffers well and loves well; there is a daily *fiat*; and there is a *fiat* for every moment, no matter how seemingly small. For each of those moments contains the epic dimension of his kingdom in you:

> Let it be to me according to your word.

5

And the angel departed
from her (Luke 1:38)

The curtain falls; the tableau breaks. The angel, mission accomplished, sidles off or simply disappears. The girl remains alone, the fact of what has taken place still exploding within her. How long did she stand there, motionless? In deepest prayer she may have remained there an hour. We cannot know what she felt.

> And the angel departed from her.

In one sense those words speak of abandonment and desolation. God's colorful messenger has gone. And, one might suppose then, his way of communicating—startling, direct, ready with an answer—is gone too. For the rest of her earthly life, Mary, like us, sits on the other side of the veil in darkness.

You see, love, she isn't so different from you. Scripture doesn't tell us she had any more angelic visitations (although of course we can't know for sure). What we can know is that she followed her Son through his mission and witnessed his horrible death. I would like to venture that God sent her a consoling angel the night before his Passion. He sent such an angel to Our Lord in the Garden of Gethsemane; I believe, in his mercy, he would not have let Our Lady shiver that awful, sleepless night alone—but we simply cannot know. Despite the city of God within her, despite her eminent relationship with the Son of God, Mary remained a mortal woman who, with the other apostles, prayed for the coming of the Holy Spirit. She walked the road in prayer and faith.

Yet, the afternoon of the Annunciation, when she eventually blinked and rubbed her eyes after the angel's departure, she was changed: wounded. I use the word "wounded" not because God's touch hurts, necessarily, but because of the way he changes us by entering into us. And Mary was certainly the *most* penetrated by God.

Would it surprise you to learn that you, too, have been wounded by God?

You receive Communion, and this is his regular way of wounding you, burrowing into you, remaining with you. In the most literal and physical way, you are touched by God every Sunday. If your heart is open, even a fraction, to grace (and I suspect that it is), you cannot fail to be wounded by him—that is, changed.

"OK, so why do I need to pray when he's inside me and already knows everything I'm thinking?" you would sometimes quibble when you were little.

Once, when I was tired, I replied, "OK, don't say your prayers. It's up to you."

And you caught my hand tightly and said, "Don't go. Let's say them like we always say them."

You sometimes slouch in front of him and yawn at Bible readings. But you screw your eyes tight when we have something especially serious to pray for, and you wrestle your arms out from under the covers to cross yourself before you go to sleep. In turn, I can only guess that he keeps quiet, keeps vigil, surprises you at times with peace, or even a sense of his presence. He answers certain prayers in a way that is not obviously required in the context of global events or salvation history but illustrates something to you. And then he falls quiet again.

Like Jacob in the Old Testament, you are wrestling God.

Jacob wrestled an angel all through the night, but just when he was winning the match, the angel struck him on the hip bone, leaving him with a limp. The angel renamed him, and blessed him too. Jacob was in no doubt that he had had an encounter with God. He was made new and given the name, Israel; his change was visible in his limp. Mary's story, though different in obvious ways, bears some similarity. She had her own little wrestle with the angel (questioning him, if you remember, and not being trounced for it), and she too is touched physically; her very flesh is transformed. Jacob walks off with a limp; she walks off with what will become a bump. Both are changed, their missions beginning.

I want to tell you another story that's not from Scripture, a story about a patient I nursed for a few hours a long time ago. She was brought into the acute psy-

chiatric ward in a state of wild psychosis. Her hair
was matted and stood up around her head like a lion's
mane. Her eyes were unfocused and ferocious. It took
a team of nurses to wrestle her into the secure room,
which was a box with three padded walls and one reinforced glass wall. My job was to sit outside the room
and observe her to make sure she didn't injure herself.

Eventually the medication would take her down. Till
then, she threw herself against the walls and glass, and
when she saw my quiet vigil her rage intensified. She
screamed that she would disembowel me with a knife
when she got near me. She jeered at me and tormented
me—about my body, my color, my hair. I wanted to
convey to her, mutely through glass, concern and kindness. I knew that most of the seasoned nurses would
simply pick up the newspaper for a task like this (and
looking back, I understand that: this crisis would pass;
till then she was in no state for any kind of therapeutic
relationship).

But I was a student and believed passionately, perhaps naïvely, that any interaction could help. So I tried
to look sympathetic, though when she became even
more enraged by my friendly smile, I made my expression neutral. By then, I think I was shaking—it was
hard not to be frightened at the sight of this crazed
woman planning my death—but I suffocated my in-
stinctive, retaliatory anger and sat very still. I knew that
picking up a newspaper would enrage her even more,
and there was something in me that wanted to do that,
to hit back with an act of indifference, a show of my

liberty. But I kept still. Somehow the shift passed. I don't remember whether she fell asleep on the floor under the influence of antipsychotic medication (probably) or whether I left her still furious when my replacement arrived.

Anyway, she was not assigned to me as a patient, and I didn't see her again—until one day, towards the end of my stint on the ward, a woman in a sharp tweed suit and heels, her long hair sleekly tied back, arrived at the nurses' station. She laughed merrily when she saw my expression, and held out her hand. "You don't remember me, do you?" It was the wild woman in the box. Her eyes were focused and kind. "I came back to say thank you. You were great that day. You took it all. You never flinched." Her transformation was so abrupt it had the essence of a parable, though then I couldn't see what the meaning might be.

Now I see the woman's desperate, sick fury as akin to all of us when we yell at God and accuse him of not listening and not being there. Mankind has also threatened to kill him and has tried to do so in various ways, whether by intellectual posturing or by the nihilism of evil. Like the woman behind the reinforced glass, we stand no chance of ever harming him. It is, of course, inappropriate to compare myself to God. But we are invited to compare ourselves to Christ, to imitate him even. My taking that small wound was, in itself, Christlike. It was not heroic, and it cost me nothing much. But the strength of a parable lies in what it signifies.

God wounds us (which is another way of saying he loves us); he, in the form of Christ, is wounded by us (this, again, is love); in turn we are called upon to be wounded by others (which is another way of saying we must love).

> You shall love the Lord your God with all your heart, and with all your soul, and with all your strength, and with all your mind; and your neighbor as yourself. (Lk 10:27)

Loving our neighbor isn't always easy. Those who are neediest are often the least attractive. They might smell bad, or just be bad tempered. They may not glow with gratitude when we hand them a sandwich. They may not do what we consider the "right thing" with the money we give them, or the food—just like we don't always do the right thing with Christ's gift of sacrifice and salvation to us. It's only through yielding to such Christlike wounds that our relationship with others can be divinized. It's giving when giving is difficult, and expecting nothing in return (Lk 6:35).

When we receive God in the Eucharist, we're also called upon to receive each other—to upset the smooth waters of our own impenetrability and let someone touch us or be touched by us. God does that: he opens us. By our overwhelming love for him he leads us gently into the necessity of loving others made in his image. The Eucharistic wound that you receive regularly, allows Christ's divinity to pour into you, if you will let it. It will keep you wounded by God, and in turn ready to be wounded by your fellow man.

Mary walked away from the scene of the Annunciation knowing that what she had experienced would have ramifications *beyond herself.* Her own wounds—the seven sorrows—are intricately connected to the sign that is Jesus, which in turn will reveal "thoughts out of many hearts" (Lk 2:35). Jacob, as he limped away, must have known that this was about more than just him. In a similar way, in the sublime privacy of the Eucharist, we are, paradoxically, united to all men in the body of Christ. We are invited to suffer for them, as he did.

When you were eight I read you the story of how people crowded into a house seeking the healing of Jesus, and one paralyzed man couldn't get in, so his friends took the roof off to let him down on his stretcher (Lk 5:18–20). You asked me, "Didn't the people whose house it was mind about their roof?" I love that you thought of that, and the dust and mess that would have been left behind. I laughed at the thought of the family staring at the sky through their roof when everyone had gone home. I wonder how peeved they were. But perhaps they weren't. Perhaps Christ's closeness, the closeness of his wounds to come, made them understand and even rejoice in their own wound taken for this paralyzed man.

But remember, please, that being wounded does not mean being abused, or physically hurt by those who would claim to love you. It does not mean putting yourself in harm's way. There was reinforced glass between me and the woman in the box. While some may be called to heroism, I am your mother, and mothers never ask for that. Remember that God's love for you —and my love for you—must ignite a healthy love of self and responsibility to self. Your body and soul are infinitely precious, and the wounds I am speaking of are in Christ and in love. They are the mother's wounds of sleeplessness, looking after an ill child; the nurse's wounds of carrying on in the face of insults; the missionary's wounds of poverty and discomfort. They are not the wounds of a person who lets her husband hit her, for example. That kind of abuse is not the healing wrestling of love and sacrifice; that is cooperating with sin and destruction.

Discernment of whether we are called to choose self-sacrifice or whether we should fight back or walk away may be one of the hardest tasks we face—and often it corresponds, it seems to me, to whether we are called to save another, in ways small or unimaginably large.

> Greater love has no man than this, that a man lay down his life for his friends. (Jn 15:13)

No, I am not worried about your wrestling with God, and the way you sometimes cast a baleful eye at the sky. This is the sign of a relationship with God more vivid than that had by many regularly present in the pews. Your frustrations and demanding to be heard are no different from the psalmist's.

Why do you stand afar off, O LORD? (Ps 10:1)

But yes, you have been touched by God, and so have
I. And so was Mary. We are all deliciously wounded
by him in various ways.

And yet . . .

~

Angels are (mostly) invisible, and God is (mostly)
silent.

As Mary's pregnancy progressed, I often wonder
how quiet God was in her prayer. Would he have felt
distant to her even as he himself, in the tiny form of
his Son, was closer to her than he would ever be to
anyone? Or did he favor her with a steady sense of his
presence? We cannot say. There are saints and mystics
who seem to have experienced God in prayer with
great vividness for years. Then there are those, like
Saint Teresa of Calcutta, who after receiving direct inspirations from God, suffered years of what we call
"the dark night".

Most people know periods of prayer that seem futile,
like talking into a disconnected phone. After all the experiences we may have had—prayers answered, a sense
of his presence, an easy warmth in ordinary prayer—
it may seem as though someone put the lights on in a
bar at the end of the evening and turned off the music.

Coldness, nothing.

I lost you only once (you were probably too small
to remember). I was picking plums from the tree and

handing them to you to put in the basket on the ground. Then I told you to stay put while I climbed to the top of the ladder to reach the highest branches. When I was as high as I could go I looked down to wave to you, but you were gone. I could see the whole garden from where I was, into every corner. You weren't there. I felt giddy. As I made a move to climb back down the ladder, I felt something behind me: it was you. You had followed me up and were gripping on for dear life. You were so close I could see everything but you.

This, too, is part of your relationship with God: sometimes he is so close, you cannot see him. Sometimes we have to take a moment to stop flailing and scouring the horizon for God or spurious solutions to our problems, to be still and know him (Ps 46:10). More: to know he is within us.

But there are times he seems to recede from us irrevocably, and we cannot understand why. Dark nights are very common—to religious on intense spiritual journeys, and to ordinary people who suddenly cannot find him—and they often follow a glorious day, a time when God shows us his obliging presence, as he did for Jonah when he grew a bush overnight to shade him in the intense heat of Nineveh.

There are times in a life of prayer when God obliges in such a way—obstacles are removed, trains arrive as you step onto the platform, people you pray for are healed of terrible illnesses. In the thick of a time just like that, my friend Sam and I began to pray for the conversion of her cousin Rebecca, who did not believe. More, Rebecca was contemptuous about religion. If Sam brought up the subject of faith, she would say, "Don't start on me!" But she had much need of God. Rebecca had been addicted to drugs for many years and had two children by different men; both children had been taken away from her. Sam, living in a very cramped apartment herself, could give little material help, and we decided that the best thing to do was to pray for Rebecca's conversion: that she would be able to come off drugs for good and that she would be able to look after her ten-year-old son herself (the other child, a baby, had already been adopted; Rebecca had already lost her).

The word "God" was so sensitive, so disparaged, that Sam could not bring herself to say it aloud in front of her cousin. But the pain in the family grew— through visits home from the son in care, visits denied, Rebecca overdosing on medication and other crises— and Sam prayed. In a bar, after some years, Rebecca, fresh from rehab but still barely functioning in life, turned to Sam in desperation and said, "I may have to up my medication."

Sam steeled herself and answered, "You might. But why don't you pray too?"

I heard about that exchange in two different ways. The first time was that same evening when Sam called me to tell me how brave she had been. The second time was five years later, when Rebecca, having read the story of my conversion, wrote me a long letter to tell me about hers. She wrote about being in the bar with Sam and said simply, "By the time I left the bar and reached the bus stop, I knew that God existed."

The letter went on to detail vividly the graces, signs, and consolations that she had since received in the immense difficulty of her life. How Sam and I rejoiced! We turned our gaze to God and thanked him. Our prayers seemed lit, connected, inspired.

As Rebecca's troubles deepened, it became clear that her boyfriend Rob also needed a change of heart. He was, understandably, overwhelmed at the scale of chaos and pain in Rebecca's life, and he wasn't at all happy about being a stepfather to such a disturbed child. "We need to pray for his conversion too," I told Sam. And so we began, earnestly and industriously, and in what seemed a very short period of time, Rob, who had had a totally unreligious upbringing, began to attend church. Soon he was expounding the Gospel to workmates and at the local bar. During his time off he could be found praying in the fields or painting images of the Cross or Jesus Christ. He began to want to be a father to Rebecca's son, and once again Sam and I danced a jig, swung our eyes to heaven, and rejoiced.

But there began to be a reckless power in what I felt. It was as if we could pray for anything and it would be answered directly and in just the way I expected. And then, just as God killed the bush sheltering Jonah, he seemed to stop answering our prayers.

Rebecca's older child was, by now, in his teens. With no prospect, still, of moving back home, he began to self-harm. There were late-night calls from police and psychiatric hospitals. Just as soon as Rebecca miraculously seemed to have her life together, something else would happen—she would become depressed or start hanging out with her old drug buddies. Even when she eventually stabilized, she couldn't quite bring herself to say that she was ready to look after her son. He, in turn, was posting desperate messages on Facebook about being alone, abandoned. He became paranoid and started drinking. Prayer became exhausting. "Do we just say it and leave it with God?" Sam asked me. "Or do we toil and groan aloud and roar at heaven?"

I said I didn't know. It was the first time in my relationship with God that I felt ignored and bewildered. It wouldn't take much to fix this, not for him! He had been listening so closely to our prayers!

I wonder if Mary ever petitioned God in the way that we did, through the course of Jesus' life. When the Holy Family was exiled in Egypt, did she ever pray to go home as soon as possible? Did she beg that her boy be kept safe? Did she cry out for his suffering to be miraculously averted as they nailed him to the cross? We know that Our Lord himself asked God to "remove this chalice." But he added, "Nevertheless not my will, but yours, be done" (Lk 22:42). Therefore, it seems likely and *human* that Mary would have prayed for a diminishment of pain. But, like her Son, this would have been coupled with absolute compliance with and trust in the divine will. The essence of Mary's prayer had to be trust. It is one thing to ask; it is another to organize life and think we know better than God.

> Who has directed the Spirit of the LORD, or as his counselor has instructed him? (Is 40:13)

Back home in Italy I began to see the complexity of Sam and Rebecca's family and my own—how faults and sins, even from generations before, choke us and create lethal consequences. There was suffering to be done, and though it seemed particularly hard that most of it was being done by a child, perhaps what God had helped us to see was the increasing nearness of Christ through prayer. Who knows how our constant petitions may be breaking that child's darkness; who knows how many hearts are being changed. But it is possible that we will not know any easily recognizable divine intervention soon, or even in this life. The only thing I feel sure of is that God wants us to carry on praying.

There are times in the spiritual life when it is time to grow up. Sometimes you cannot pray for something and have it arrive like a gift; the days of simple exchange may seem to be over. God is careful with us; he knows us well. How quickly we can come to feel powerful, as though we control God. But his response can be too large for us to understand. He sees far beyond what we can see, and his business is all in the gathering of us to himself. When it feels as though God is indifferent to your suffering, meditate on the

Passion of Christ. Remember his atrocious suffering, and also the suffering of his Mother. Think of Mary Magdalene's tears when she went to find him in the tomb and he had gone.

After the Crucifixion and before the Resurrection, the thread of trust must have been pulled to its limit and must have snapped for many. The very earth sank, deadened. The sky was leaden and impenetrable. God himself had died. From all of this, he rose and called her name. But in those "in-between" hours, I believe he took that sense of abandonment and desolation and uses it with his Son's suffering for our redemption, because those feelings spell our utter dependence on him.

Eternally, we, like Mary Magdalene, are the weeping lover who is slowly raising her head, almost unbelievingly but with unimaginable joy, at the sight of the Beloved who has returned. Faith is this: pain at our aloneness, intertwined with the sweet hope we have for his coming. In this life we must keep these two conflicting feelings close. One feeds the other. When it seems as though your prayers are not being answered, remember how he—beyond all expectation and any reasonable hope—called her name.

∿

But we are prey to darkness. It is one thing to feel bewilderment at the ways of God or to feel despair at the events of our lives. It is another to feel what I'll call the psychological dark night.

It is one of life's ironies that mental illness can impede prayer. I say "mental illness", but that shouldn't make you or anyone think they can shelve those words and imagine they are not relevant to them. "Mental illness" sounds scary and formal. In reality, most of us—at some point—will succumb to the fluctuations of neurotransmitters and hormones that are an inescapable fact of life.

If you are anything like me, you will be conscious of hormones affecting how you see the world, on a cyclical basis. This is not always a bad thing. If I weep at the news at certain times of the month, it seems to me a saner response than a reaction of indifference ("Blessed are those who mourn" [Mt 5:4]). This hyperempathy is a very feminine trait, and in many ways we should be grateful for it: it can sanctify us if it leads us to prayer and self-sacrifice.

But then, there are the times that hormones or neurotransmitters can become dark, distorting forces that seem to extinguish all the lights of mind and body. In that state, climbing the stairs can be exhausting, cooking dinner completely unmanageable. There are times when *doing* is beyond us, and prayer—particularly prayers like the Rosary—takes some doing.

When we cannot find the door handle to access God in the dark, and lose any sense of where he is or whether he is there at all, our eyes are dimmed, our limbs seem filled with sand, our heart folds up. We cannot bring ourselves to pray. Of course, the devil loves this; it is his opportunity. We feel worthless, inadequate, hopeless. The peace that Christ gives us is strangled in this pit.

Don't forget that the devil is the father of lies, and when we are weak, hungry, tired, frightened, or angry, we are most likely to believe those lies. They will always involve a destruction of the self: "You are no good, you are not attractive, you are a failure, everyone else is better than you. What kind of a girl or boy are you? No one really likes you, no one really loves you." All of these thoughts are lies. They deconstruct fundamental truths about you and about everyone: God made you good because everything that God makes is good; God loves you; even if you make mistakes. There is no situation so dire that it cannot be rectified by the immense mercy and love of God. Still, despair feeds on despair, and dulls us to his presence.

Remember, in whatever circumstance: you have to *choose* God.

> There are two paths, one of life and one of death, and the difference is great between the two paths.[1]

If you are ever terribly down, you will know that it is a little like being drugged (your brain chemistry is altered, so it really is like you've taken something mind-altering). Being low saps your energy and ability to choose and do the right things—like eating well, being truthful, working, walking, praying. But the choices

---

[1] *The Didache: The Teaching of the Twelve Apostles.*

remain. We all have to *choose* to be well and to *choose* to be holy. Depression and discouragement just make it more difficult. (Some would say that severe depression makes it so difficult that there is no choice. Nevertheless, every second of our lives presents a choice to be alert to; and in my personal and limited clinical experience, reminding someone of his free will in mental illness can be a defining step.)

If you ever suffer from depression (or its natural cousins: grief, heartbreak, trauma), you must use every ounce of your strength to ignore the lies it tells you and to galvanize every cell of yourself to do the right thing. And then move forward in tiny steps. Tinier steps. Moment by moment. Every second is anchored in trust; our Mother tells us so as she waits under the cross. Perhaps she still hears Gabriel's words: "Do not be afraid."

If only we knew how heroic this kind of struggle is! The darkness that we are in at these times is the "pit clos[ing] its mouth" over us (Ps 69:15). It is an intimation of God's absence (that is, hell). It is an affliction that has no obvious meaning. But in it we are intimately united with Christ on the cross.

My God, my God, why have you forsaken me? (Mt 27:46)

Never has God seemed so far away; never has he been so near. In that blackest place, even talking can sap the breath.

If there is one word you should always try to say, it

must be his most holy name. Remember how we form
the city of God within us. Remember that what is spo-
ken is strengthened. Name him. Physically move your
lips to say his name (and I know that in true misery
even this can feel like a physical feat). Language is powerful: it shows what is there. When we feel empty as
the formless void before all creation (Gen 1:1), speaking the name of Our Lord Jesus Christ lights a shape
that is already biding within us. He was always there;
he *is* there. Speaking his name strengthens our knowledge of this and brings him closer. When even prayer
seems like too much, just say his name. And again. It
might not seem much. It might not seem enough. But
it *is*. Say his name. Listen for his listening.

~

He *is* listening. I imagine God walking around the
empty Garden of Eden in the evening, and Christ walking in an empty garden the morning of the Resurrection. God is waiting for his children to come home—
he is a father like the father of the prodigal son parable:
he wants us with him.

"But *why* do I have to go to Mass?"

Your question still rings in my ears. Remember that
through dark nights, the Mass is there. Through depression, the Mass is there. Through death and loss,
the Mass is there—and Christ saves and transforms all
that we are grieving for. In happiness, the Mass is there
—and happiness infused with the divine is longer last-

ing, a heady yet steady joy. In love and marriage, the Mass is there. It is there to connect us with heaven, to touch us and allow us moments of communion with the Trinity and all the saints and angels. The Mass is your answer to seemingly unanswered prayers: it draws you to Christ, which is the ultimate answer to any and every prayer.

The bliss of the Mass is also this: it precisely *doesn't* require philosophical expertise. God did all the thinking for you. He gave you a place (the church building), and he gave you a time (when Mass is offered), and he gave you your sacrifice (not a bird or a bull but the Body and Blood of his only Son). He asks only that you come. And then he lets you into eternity and makes the death of his Son—which is over and done with, once and for all—something that is always, that counts for always, that is happening now.[2]

But there's something else. You know that we offer the sacrifice of Our Lord Jesus Christ on the altar. But God also wants *you*. Since Adam and Eve's exit from Eden, sacrifice has been our central way of communicating with God. And in the Mass, he is asking for *you*. When you offer up Christ, you are also asked to offer up the whole of yourself to God (Rom 12:1)—your happiness as well as your sorrow, everything that you are. Listen: this is the Father calling you back to himself. You are doing what our first parents did not,

---

[2] Joseph Cardinal Ratzinger, *The Spirit of the Liturgy* (San Francisco: Ignatius Press, 2000), p. 56.

ultimately, do—you are recognizing that you belong to him.

As much as you worry that you don't do things right, there is *nothing* in you that is not pleasing to God when you hand it to him—humiliations, losses, sins, accomplishments, or ecstasy. You do not lose those things by giving them to him; rather, in his hands, they are transformed, given meaning, and made holy. God is the ultimate artist, and as with any master, there is not one expression of yours that he will not delight in perfecting.

What I said to you as a nine-year-old is no different from what I will say to you as an adult: "Just open the door."

∽

Recently, when a six-year-old friend had a meltdown and her mother turned to me in desperation, I asked you (now so grown up) how you dealt with feelings of despair. You listed a few things, and then I asked, "Do you pray?"

"No!" you snapped. Then, as I turned to go, you said, "I do pray, but it's none of your business."

It's one thing I'm learning as a mother: a child's religious sense grows with him like his sexuality or his need for independence. Even through writing these pages, I have witnessed your faith form in you—a new seriousness, a protectiveness of God and prayer. Time takes care of many things (after all, God is in the steady rush of time as well as out of it), but I realize, too, that writing has been a way of praying: a total focus of attention on God and you; a handing of you to him.

Your relationship with him is uniquely your own, and I can't know what goes on between you. I can only watch and continue to pray as you draw closer to him, or perhaps pull away. The only sureness I have is that you do now know him; this delights me and brings me great relief.

As we say the Rosary down the road in summer, even the deep red oleander blossoms look like drops of his blood. Even the tops of telegraph poles look like crosses. Even the birdsong speaks of the emptiness of the tomb and the beauty of his word to Mary Magdalene. Nothing has ever been the same again. Tonight you skipped ahead in your red polka-dot dress, lighting the dusk. Did you know that you take God out into the world? You are a living tabernacle where Christ dwells. He is in your heart, your eyes and ears. He is in the scattering and gathering of starlings in a tree, and the emerald of the pines. He is beyond the endlessness of the sea. He is in the line of homeless in the tunnel by the piazza. In coffee bars and passing nuns. There is nothing in which Christ will not speak if you will only listen.

Soon you will be confirmed. For a long time you couldn't decide which saint's name you would take, and in the end it had to be two: Bernadette-Jacinta. Great grandchild of Sardinian shepherds, these two saints even look like your sisters. "Hail Mary, Hail

Mary, Hail Mary,'' little Jacinta would chant, to cut the Rosary short. You liked that.

Just as we are asked to imitate Christ, we are asked to imitate our Blessed Mother. The Annunciation was the ultimate watershed. But every moment in your life is just such a choice; your angel is constantly holding his breath for your answer. As we say the full angelic salutation down the street, I think that this is why we say it so many times: so that we never let go of the tipping point which allows Christ into our life and we always remember how very alone we could have been if Mary's angel had not come for us all.

Works Mentioned

Anonymous. *The Way of a Pilgrim* and *The Pilgrim Continues His Way*. Translated by Helen Bacovcin. New York: Image Books, Doubleday, 2003.

Benedict XVI. Homily, Saint Peter's Basilica, September 29, 2007. http://w2.vatican.va/content/benedict -xvi/en /homilies/2007/documents/hf_ben-xvi_hom _20070929_episc-ordinations.html.

Benedict XVI. *Jesus of Nazareth: From the Baptism in the Jordan to the Transfiguration*. San Francisco: Ignatius Press, 2008.

Catherine Benincasa (Catherine of Siena). *Letters of Catherine Benincasa*. Translated by Vida D. Scudder. Project Gutenberg EBook. February, 2005.

Catherine of Siena. *The Dialogue of the Seraphic Virgin Catherine of Siena*. Translated by Algar Thorold. CreateSpace Independent Publishing Platform, 2015. Kindle.

De Caussade, Jean-Pierre. *Abandonment to Divine Providence*. Translated by John Beevers. New York: Image Books, 1975.

Didache: The Teaching of the Twelve Apostles. Translated by Charles Hoole. Trunk Books, Amazon Media, 2018.

Houselander, Caryll. *A Rocking-Horse Catholic.* Pickle Partners Publishing, 2016.

John Paul II. Apostolic Exhortation *Familiaris Consortio*, November 22, 1981. http://w2.vatican.va/con tent/john-paul-ii/en/apost_exhortations/documents /hf_jp-ii_exh_19811122_familiaris-consortio.html.

Julian. *Revelations of Divine Love Recorded by Julian, Anchoress at Norwich.* Translated by Grace Warrack. Project Gutenberg EBook, September 2, 2016.

Kowalska, Maria Faustina. *Diary of Saint Maria Faustina Kowalska: Divine Mercy in My Soul.* Stockbridge, Mass.: Marian Press, 2006.

Murray, Paul. *I Loved Jesus in the Night: Teresa of Calcutta; A Secret Revealed.* London: Darton, Longman and Todd Ltd, 2008.

"Nel mondo ma non nel mondo—Scienza e vita (1)—Chiara Corbella Petrillo", YouTube, uploaded October 8, 2012, https://www.youtube.com/watch?v =ZX-gFbtC2dU.

Paul VI. General Audience, June 26, 1974. https://w2. vatican.va/content/paul-vi/it/audiences/1974/docu ments/hf_p-vi_aud_19740626.html.

Protoevangelium of James, quoted in Ratzinger and von Balthasar. *Mary: The Church at the Source.* Translated by Adrian Walker. San Francisco: Ignatius Press, 2005.

Ratzinger, Joseph Cardinal and Hans Urs von Balthasar. *Mary: The Church at the Source.* Translated by Adrian Walker. San Francisco: Ignatius Press, 2005.

Ratzinger, Joseph Cardinal. *The Spirit of the Liturgy.* San Francisco: Ignatius Press, 2000.

Teresa of Avila. *The Life of Saint Teresa of Avila by Herself.* Translated by J. M. Cohen. London: Penguin Books, 1957.

Troisi Simone and Paccini Cristiana. *Chiara Corbella Petrillo: A Witness to Joy.* Translated by Charlotte J. Fasi. Manchester, New Hampshire: Sophia Institute Press, 2015. Kindle.